THE MILITARY AND THE
NIGERIAN STATE, 1966-1993

THE MILITARY AND THE NIGERIAN STATE, 1966-1993

A Study of the Strategies of Political Power Control

Adegboyega Isaac Ajayi

Africa World Press, Inc.

P.O. Box 1892
Trenton, NJ 08607

P.O. Box 48
Asmara, ERITREA

Dedicated to God Almighty for His protection and sustenance; and to the National Democratic Coalition (NADECO) and other progressive forces that assisted in the liberation of Nigeria from the clutches of military dictatorship.

Africa World Press, Inc.

P.O. Box 1892
Trenton, NJ 08607

P.O. Box 48
Asmara, ERITREA

Copyright © 2007 Adegboyega Isaac Ajayi
First Printing 2007

Book and Cover design: Saverance Publishing Services

Library of Congress Cataloging-in-Publication Data

Ajayi, Gboyega.
  The military and the Nigerian state, 1966-1993 : a study of the strategies of political power control / Adegboyega Isaac Ajayi.
    p. cm.
  Includes bibliographical references and index.
  ISBN 1-59221-568-8 (hb) -- ISBN 1-59221-569-6 (pb)
  1. Nigeria--Politics and government--1960- 2. Nigeria--History--Civil War, 1967-1970. 3. Nigeria. Nigerian Army--Political activity. 4. Civil-military relations--Nigeria--History--20th century. 5. Military government--Nigeria--History--20th century. 6. Power (Social sciences)--Nigeria--History--20th century. I. Title.

DT515.8.A545 2007
966.905'3--dc22

                    2007006417

Table of Contents

List of Abbreviations

ABN	Association for Better Nigeria
AFCA	Armed Forces Consultative Assembly
AG	Action Group
ALF	African Leadership Forum
ASCON	Administrative Staff College of Nigeria
ASUU	Academic Staff Union of (Nigerian) Universities
AVM	Air Vice Marshal
BLP	Better Life Programme
CA	Constituent Assembly
CBN	Central Bank of Nigeria
CAN	Christian Association of Nigeria
CD	Campaign for Democracy
CDC	Constitution Drafting Committee
CDHR	Committee For The Defence of Human Rights
CDS	Centre for Democratic Studies
CLO	Civil Liberties Organisation
DIFRRI	Directorate of Food, Roads and Rural Infrastructures
ECOMOG	Economic Community of West African States' Monitoring Group
ECOWAS	Economic Community of West African States

List of Tables

NRC	National Republican Convention
NUR	National Union of Railwaymen
NWC	National War College
NYSC	National Youth Service Corps
OAU	Organization of African Unity
OIC	Organization of Islamic Conference
PRC	Provisional Ruling Council
PZ	Patterson and Zochonis
RWAFF	Royal West African Frontier Force
SAP	Structural Adjustment Programme
SDP	Social Democratic Party
SMC	Supreme Military Council
TCPC	Technical Committee on Privatisation and Commercialisation
TRADOC	Training and Doctrine Command
UAC	United African Company
UNO	United Nations' Organisation
UPN	Unity Party of Nigeria
WAFF	West African Frontier Force
WAI	War Against Indiscipline
WNTV	Western Nigeria Television

FEDECO	Federal Electoral Commission
FHA	Federal Housing Authority
FMG	Federal Military Government
GCFR	Grand Commander of The Federal Republic
GNPP	Great Nigeria Peoples' Party
HRD	House of Representatives' Debates
IAP	Industrial Arbitration Panel
IBB	Ibrahim Badamosi Babangida
IDB	Islamic Development Bank
ING	Interim National Government
MAMSER	Mass Mobilisation for Social Justice and Economic Recovery
NANS	National Association of Nigerian Students
NAI	National Archives Ibadan
NBC	National Broadcasting Commission
NCNC	National Council of Nigerian Citizens
NDA	Nigerian Defence Academy
NDSC	Nigerian Defence and Security Council
NEC	National Electoral Commission
NERFUND	National Economic Recovery Fund
NIC	National Industrial Court
NICON	National Insurance Corporation of Nigeria
NIPSS	National Institute of Policy and Strategic Studies
NLC	Nigeria Labour Congress
NNDP	Nigeria National Democratic Party
NOA	National Orientation Agency
NPC	National Population Commission
NPP	Nigeria Peoples' Party
NPN	National Party of Nigeria
NPSA	Nigeria Political Science Association

Foreword

The military has dominated the Nigerian political space since it first came to power in 1966. Today, although Nigeria claims to be a democracy, its president is a former military general who came to power in a coup in the 1970s. Outside of official political power, the military also includes many men who have stolen substantial amounts of public money, and who continue to use this stolen money to acquire political influence. In moments of great political upheaval, as in the current circumstances, there is always the fear of a possible coup.

Dr. Adegboyega Isaac Ajayi, a scholar and university administrator, has focused on a major era in the history of Nigeria, namely, when the military dominated the country for over two decades. His aim is to examine why the military stayed in power for so long and the concomitant damages. He has fulfilled his intellectual agenda in a brilliant manner.

The fascinating chapters reveal the conflicts of power, the reckless ambition to stay in power, the pursuit of greed, and the reckless disregard for the interests of the majority of the Nigerian population. In an attempt to sustain themselves in power, the military has had no respect for laws and lives. Their actions reveal barbarism at its most primitive. They created instability and chaos, using violence to sustain themselves in power.

The victims are Nigerians who have been denied the opportunity to experiment with a truly democratic order, pursue goals of sustainable development, and create viable civil societies. Rather than see the robust articulation of the public good, we see strate-

Preface

This book, which focuses on the military and the Nigerian state, is a revised version of a doctoral thesis that I presented to the university of Ibadan, Ibadan Nigeria in December, 2001. It establishes the circumstances of military incursion into politics and examines the civil war and how it enhanced the military's control of political power. It highlights and analyses the strategies which the military rulers consciously employed to monopolise political power in Nigeria between 1966 and 1993 when the General Babangida regime handed over power to an Interim Government.

The study relies on archival materials, findings and documents from research institutes, private and government publications, periodicals, magazines and other relevant secondary materials. The book concludes that: a deliberate 'corrective regime' posturing; the politics of patronage and subordination; the employment of coerciveand repressive methods, militarisation and guided transition programmes were used (with varying degrees of success) by different military regimes to prolong the military's hold on political power.

On the surface, some of these strategies look well-intentioned and patriotically motivated. But in actual fact, as the book argues, they were deviously manipulated to prolong military rule. In the process the military organization and the civil society were adversely affected. In fact, by 1993 the country had been brought to the brink of disintegration. The cumulative effect of prolonged military rule and particularly General Babangida's gies of evil, ingenious military methods, destructive tactics, and a society permanently at war with itself. Dr. Ajayi presents images of conflicts, threats to peace, and the destruction of a "profitable country."

This book has filled a major vacuum in the literature. It is a major contribution to the study of the Nigerian military and its intervention in politics. We can see from this study the nature of political turmoil in a mismanaged country, the pestilence of power, the state as the enemy of the people, and crude authoritarianism.

For surviving the military, the Nigerian masses deserve to be congratulated. Dr. Ajayi celebrates anti-military organizations. Although the civilian rule that followed in 1999 has been a gross disappointment, the struggles to terminate military rule should be praised.

The future of Nigeria is unpredictable. It is abundantly clear that politics is no more than a grand orchestration of a cabal—military and civilians—motivated by the narrow desire of acquiring power for its sake. Nigerian leaders do not care about law and order. We are beginning to have entrenched forces, men who lived and thrived in the era described in this book. To this ruthless cabal, democracy is about the use of violence, the destruction of opponents, and the looting of treasuries. In the configuration of Nigerian politics, Dr. Ajayi has given us a major diagnosis of a sick era. The guns used by the military have now been handed over to their civilian successors to implement a gun-barrel democracy.

Toyin Falola
Fellow of the Historical Society of Nigeria

I wish to express my gratitude to all those who contributed, in one form or the other, to the successful completion of this book. I am particularly grateful to the staff of the Hezekiah Oluwasanmi Library, Obafemi Awolowo University, Ile-Ife, Kenneth Dike Memorial Library, University of Ibadan, and the National Archives, Ibadan, for granting me access to relevant documents, books and journals in their custody. I am also grateful to the officials of the National Orientation Agency;

Centre for Democratic Studies, Abuja; Friedrich Ebert Foundation, University of Lagos; and, the African Leadership Forum, Otta, for making available to me government and private publications which served as part of my source materials for this book.

I would like to thank my supervisor, Dr. G.O. Oguntomisin who read through the work several times and made very useful suggestions on how to improve it. I am quite appreciative of his encouragement and guidance. I am also grateful to late Dr. Kola Olufemi, Head, Department of Political Science, Obafemi Awolowo University, Ile-Ife, Dr. Akin Alao of the Department of History of the same institution, Dr. Tayo Adesina and Dr. Victor Edo, of the Department of History, University of Ibadan; and, Dr. Wale Osisanwo of the Department of English, Adeyemi College of Education, Ondo and Professor Toyin Falola of the department of History University of Texas at Austin, for sparing the time to go through the work.

My special thanks to Miss Esther Akinkoye, Mrs. Dupe Olowolagba and Mrs. M..M. Owoyemi who worked on the typing of the first and final drafts of the manuscript. I am greatly indebted to my brother, Barrister S.B. Ajayi and my sister Dr. (Mrs) A. O. Aderounmu for their financial and moral support.

Finally, I would like to express my profound gratitude to my wife, Olumuyiwa and our children, Adegboyega (Junior), Adeyinka and Akintunde for their forbearance and unflinching support at all times. The good Lord will bless all of you mightily.

Adegboyega Ajayi
Ondo, August 2006.

political machinations discredited military rule and created deep cleavages in the civil society.

In order to liberate the Nigerian state from the military's stranglehold the book argues for the withdrawal of patronage for military regimes by civilians. It is believed that no military regime can survive without the support of civilians. And that, if such support is denied, the military would be forced to remain in the barracks. Civilians would therefore have the much needed space and the right environment to fashion out a truly democratic alternative to military rule.

However, it is strongly emphasized that the only antidote to military take-over of government is good governance based on justice, fairplay and equitable distribution of national resources. It is therefore recommended that whenever power devolves on civilians they should conduct themselves and the affairs of state in such a way that they will not give the military any excuse to stage a comeback.

It is also suggested that the civilian government should take some practical steps to keep the military under control. These will include reducing the numerical strength of the military to a manageable proportion, getting the military constantly engaged in border patrols, road constructions, rescue missions and general preparation for any emergency in order to keep it gainfully employed; and, putting in place far-reaching welfare programmes that would render political adventurism less attractive. In addition, the support of influential international organizations, like the United Nations Organization, the Commonwealth of Nations, African Union and the Economic Community of West African States, must be enlisted to keep the military at bay.

The book has complemented the existing studies on military rule in Nigeria in general and has specifically exposed the strategies which the military employed to perpetuate itself in government. Fundamentally, it is a refutation of the 'corrective regime' claim and an endorsement of the increasingly popular notion of the military as a usurper of political power in Nigeria.

INTRODUCTION

The basic premise on which this study is constructed is that military rulers in Nigeria were concerned chiefly with the control and exercise of political power. In other words, governance, as far as the military was concerned, was primarily about the exercise of power, the subjection of the country and its people to authoritarian control. And, for this purpose strategies had to be evolved in order to retain power. The following questions captured the research problem:

(a) What strategies were evolved to ensure power control?
(b) To what extent did the personality of the rulers and societal idiosyncrasies affect the efficacy of the strategies?
(c) How effective were the strategies in ensuring military dominance in Nigerian politics?

The general purpose of this study is to demonstrate that the military was able to control political power for so long in post-independence Nigeria as a result of the conscious employment of certain strategies. In specific terms, the study was carried out;

(i) to identify and discuss the strategies evolved by the military rulers;
(ii) to account for the effectiveness of the strategies; and
(iii) to examine the impact of the strategies on the polity.

In the final analysis it is hoped that the outcome of the study will be a worthy addition to the expanding body of knowledge

on the dominant position of the military in post-independence Nigerian politics.

Between 1966 and 1993, Nigeria was subjected to different shades of military rule with brief periods of civilian interregnum between 1979 and 1983, and for barely three months in 1993. The usual excuse for taking over government was to sanitise the political terrain and prepare the ground for democratic governance.

In the process, the military usurped political power which it held on to tenaciously. Its possession and judicious application of the instruments of coercion and other consciously evolved strategies were of immense assistance in attaining and retaining political power.

The fact of the military's predominant position in Nigeria's politics has been documented, directly or indirectly, by many writers. But the concern in most cases has been more for advancing reasons for military intervention in politics, the performance of regimes in office and evaluation of the prospect of total military disengagement from politics. This has sometimes been done on a discriminatory epochal basis thereby creating the impression that the military regimes were markedly different from one another. Whereas, there were some common strategies that were employed (albeit with varying degrees of emphasis) by nearly all the regimes at this period. An exposition and examination of such strategies constituted the focus of this study.

A lot has been written on the 'military' and the literature keeps on expanding by the day. It is therefore practically impossible to exhaust all the available works in this field in a review. Moreover, there is a need to have a clear focus. Therefore, only works that are directly relevant to the study will be reviewed. This will be undertaken in three parts, as categorised below:

(i)   The Nature and Character of the Military Institution.
(ii) The Military and the State.
(iii) The Military and Disengagement from Politics.

In addition a section is devoted to concluding remarks on the gaps and slippages in the literature and the orientation of the present study.

THE NATURE AND CHARACTER OF THE MILITARY INSTITUTION

Our preoccupation with this theme is informed by the fact that there is a causal relationship between the nature of military institution and its political performance. Scholars of civil-military relations like Bayo Adekanye[1] and Claude Ake[2] have established the fact that the nature of military organisation tends to define military rule. There is therefore a need to understand the 'unique' nature of the institution in order to appreciate its political performance. Adekanye proceeded to identify some distinguishing properties of the military as, unitary command structure, concentration of authority, hierarchical structural relations, specialisation, penchant for discipline, continuous communication and esprit de corp[3]. Claude Ake amplified some of these properties in the following words:

a)   the organisation is a chain of command whose members are integrated in a strict relationship of subordination and superordination;

b)   it operates in a context of extreme danger – a situation which calls for highly disciplined behaviour, decisiveness and speed of operation;

c)   the organisation of the military leaves no doubt as to who is in charge in every situation;

d)   the military is necessarily authoritarian. It does not place much value on discussion, negotiation or consensus. One person decides, the other complies[4].

Thus, "when the military comes into government it cannot help acting like a fighting machine"[5]. This observation has been reinforced by Kunle Amuwo's assertion that;

Once the military as juntas, individual officers and cliques get into visible political offices the ensuing military rule becomes the pursuit of 'war', the military's primary calling. Indeed in this context politics is conceptualised as a war game while the whole country becomes an extensive and far-flung battle-field[6].

The scenario is poignantly captured in Adekanye's study of the character of the 'military as government' during the Gen. Babangida's transition period. He observed rightly that Gen. Babangida was continuously "tackling Nigeria's major organised groups or interests as if dealing with successive teams of opponents in a football game, or even warfare"[7].

But this was a no-holds-barred game in which one of the contestants – the military rulers – also doubles as the initiator of the rules of the game as well as serving as the referee or arbitrator. What is even more important is the violent (physical and psychic) nature of the game. Again, this derived from the nature of the military organisation.

It has been established that the basic property which makes the military unique is the acquired skill in the management and deployment of violence. Rapoport[8] and Feld[9] writing differently reached a similar conclusion which validates this position. Billy Dudley also conceded this property by stating that "apart from their overwhelming superiority in matters of force and violence and a special skill in the use of arms, the armed forces have no special characteristics which are not shared by other members of the community"[10]. There is no doubting the fact that military men are trained to kill and destroy perceived enemies. It is to be expected therefore that they would harbour some violent streaks which must be expressed sometimes. In situation of war such instincts temporarily find expression. But "in the absence of any visible or credible external threat the military visit their warfare instincts and prowess on the hapless and powerless civilian population"[11]. At least this has been the case in the third world countries (Nigeria inclusive) which have experienced military rule.

In Nigeria, for instance, the military relied more on violence and some short term strategies (which shall be discussed elaborately later) to gain and retain control over the state. Falola and Ihonvbere have rightly observed that it is its historical antecedent as an institution established to employ violence to sustain imperialism that puts it in the position to control and deploy at will the coercive apparatuses of the state[12]. In the process, the military in Nigeria progressively emerged as a dominant subclass. Bayo Adekanye affirmed the 'class' character of the military when he observed that it has emerged in Nigeria as "a privileged stratum"[13].

Kunle Amuwo had expressed similar views when he asserted that,

> ... the Nigerian military is a new class not necessarily in terms of ownership and production but rather to the extent that its monopoly of the paraphernalia of force and coercion permits it to define the context and content of the political game; maintain socio-political homeostasis and a conducive environment for other factions of the ruling class to accumulate some surplus and capital. The other major factions become little more than supportive edifices of the militarist state[14].

The dependent variable in the situation described above is 'power'. According to Max Weber, "power (*Macht*) is the probability that one actor within a social relationship will be in a position to carry out his own will despite resistance, regardless of the basis on which the probability rests"[15]. Thus, the control of the use of force gave the military an edge over competing social groups in gaining control over the Nigerian state.

But force alone is not enough to guarantee continued retention of power as Olufemi Taiwo has argued. According to him after attaining power through force, a military regime had to quickly "add some moral stature to itself, i.e., make itself legitimate or appear legitimate in the eyes of those it governs", if it intends "to remain in power without costly repeated challenges

to its rule"[16]. Evidently Taiwo's argument was influenced by Jean-Jacques Rousseau's dictum: "The strongest is never strong enough to be always the master unless he transforms might into right and obedience into duty"[17]. He proceeded to outline two interlocking processes through which the transformation can be achieved:

(i)   the regime which has come to power through force or the threat of force appeals to criterion *other than* force to justify its breach of the principle of legitimacy of the polity. Such appeal is meant to persuade the governed that the breach was *right*, that not to execute it would be wrong;

(ii) the citizens who are the subjects come to believe that force had been exercised on behalf of right and that the new regime does have a *right* to govern. (emphasis in the original)[18].

This partially explains military rulers' puritanic affectations and the so-called 'corrective regime' disposition at the onset of their regime. However, even when other factors came to play, force was the constant variable in the military's political machinations.

The sum total of what we have been discussing is that the nature and character of the military as an institution has a profound influence on its orientation and disposition in politics. But we also recognise the fact that the 'military in government' is also influenced by other factors that are extraneous to the organisation. We must remember that the military is part and parcel of a larger society which it must relate to accordingly in whatever capacity it finds itself.

THE MILITARY AND THE STATE

From colonial times up to the immediate post-independence period in Nigeria, the military acted as the coercive arm of government. Thus when it seized power in 1966, coercion and repression featured prominently in its handling of state affairs. At the same time social and economic factors were often employed to shore-up the regimes in power. This is reminiscent of Machiavelli's 'prince'.

Adekanye has done a number of studies[19] in which he analyzed Machiavelli's postulations and related them to the character of military rule. Of particular interest to this work is his examination of Gen. Babangida's leadership style in "The military". After a copious illustration of Gen. Babangida's 'maradonic' political juggling and intrigues, he affirmed that Babangida was "a skillful strategist; master political tactician (and) indeed the most consummate Machiavelli's prince in action on the contemporary African scene"[20]. This position has been reinforced in a doctoral dissertation put together by Adeolu Akande[21]. From the study it is apparent that Gen. Babangida deliberately cultivated a personalist leadership style and used moral, religious, ethnic and economic factors to consolidate his hold on the state in the manner of Machiavelli's prescriptions.

While it can be argued, with some measure of correctness, that other military rulers who preceded Babangida in office also used some of these factors for the same purpose, he approximated more to that conjectural "Prince". This will be validated later in this study. Suffice it to say for now that for the period covered by this study the Babangida regime outstripped other regimes in nearly all ramifications. It represented all the extremes of military rule, political intrigues and manipulations. But it ended in dismal failure because "General Babangida outsmarted himself, as his constant manipulations alienated public opinion and trust rather than uniting the citizenry behind the government, while providing the former political class the opportunity to sow the seeds of more discords and disaffection"[22]. This leads us to the examination of some works that are based on military leadership types.

A leading authority in civil-military relations, Eboe Hutchful, has identified three types of military regimes. These are the Classical, Militariat and Patrimonial regimes[23]. In a classical military regime, the military hierarchy, acting in the name of the establishment, exercises political power corporately and outside the formal political process. Governance is seen as a military assignment to be executed as such and to be terminated as soon as circumstances permit. Here military leaders would seem to

be better disposed to a quick disengagement from politics after the political arena would have been properly sanitised. This has a parallel in Amos Perlmutter's 'Arbitrator Type' military regime which would not wield political power longer than necessary [24]. Hutchful's second category (i.e. the Militariat) typifies junior officers who operate outside the military hierarchy to rule in coalition with civilians. This gives the Militariat a somewhat revolutionary character. Notable examples in Africa include Jerry Rawlings in Ghana, Thomas Sankara and Blaise Campaore in Burkina Faso, Sergeant Doe in Liberia and Jammeh in the Gambia.

The third category is typified by a patrimonial ruler who uses personal favours, reward, political patronage and clientelism to dominate the military as well as the state. A patrimonial regime is that regime in which "political power and state administration are often personalised or highly concentrated in a small group, economic resources and control devolved on the ruler, patron-client relations and rent-seeking activities gain prominence"[25].

In this situation the propensity for the leader to perpetuate himself in office is very high. Adeolu Akande has submitted that "elements of patrimonialism exist in all systems although in varying degrees. While it is dominant in some, it is residual in others"[26]. Patrimonialism seeks to describe political system having clientelistic features. According to Rene Lemarchand and Keith Legg clientelism describes a "more or less personalised relationship between actors or sets of actors commanding unequal wealth, status or influence, based on conditional loyalties and involving mutually beneficial transactions"[27]. James Scott offers a more graphic representation of the concept by describing it as "a special case of dyadic relationship in which an individual of higher socio-economic status (Patron) uses his own influence and resources to provide protection or benefit, or both, for a person of lower status (Client) who for his part, reciprocates by offering general support and assistance, including personal services to the patron" [28].

Peter Flynn identified three significant features of clientelism as follows:

(i) two parties unequal in status, wealth and influence constitute the relationship;

(ii) it is based on, and sustained by, reciprocity in the exchange of relevant goods and services, and;

(iii) it subsists on a direct face-to-face interaction[29].

But, as rightly observed by Lemarchand and Legg, patron-client relations do go beyond just two partners and can extend to formal structures like bureaucracy, political parties, corporate groups and even informal structures like cliques, reference groups, coterie, etc[30]. Clientelism is a relational concept, related to but different from ethnicity. They "refer to basically different levels of solidarity. Whereas clientelism describes a personalised relationship, ethnicity is fundamentally a group phenomenon". Richard Sandbrook has submitted that clientelism is a convenient tool for individuals to improve their situation in a setting where class consciousness is weak or not tangibly felt[31]. This partly explains its prevalence in Africa. Other contributory factors have been identified as follows:

(i) the failure of implanted alien political systems

(ii) the demands of the new African states

(iii) the ambition of the emergent rulers[32].

From the foregoing discussions we can easily appreciate why political power usurpers (like military rulers) employed patrimonialism or what we refer to as the 'politics of patronage and subordination' (later in this study)[33]. In the Nigerian context while neo-patrimonialism was common to all the military regimes that fell within the scope of our study, the Babangida regime stood out as an era of personalist rule in which political power was concentrated singularly around the person of President Babangida. He wielded such tremendous power that he loomed larger than the military and the state. It got to a point at which the regime was virtually unassailable. But, as noted previously from Adekanye, he eventually became a victim of his political machinations.

THE MILITARY AND DISENGAGEMENT FROM POLITICS

In the Nigerian context, military rule is generally considered an aberration or at best a short term expediency during which period the military men "are to take corrective measures, cure the system of its ailments, and then return power to the rightful wielders"[34]. In fact, as Anthony Kirk-Greene and Douglas Rimmer have rightly observed, after a successful coup "the question usually asked in Nigeria was not *whether* but *when* the return would be made to elected constitutional government"[35] (emphasis in the original). Dare also posited that "Nigerian military men see themselves as 'reactive interveners' ... (who) operates (sic) from the position that military rule should be kept very short and that the rightful role of the military is soldiering from the barracks"[36]. But it appears as if this conviction only operated at the level of rhetorical pronouncements for some military regimes. In other words not all the military rulers shared this conception of military rule. The experience of Generals Gowon and Babangida's regimes buttresses this position.

We can recall that Gen. Gowon had to be unseated through military coup after staying in office for nine years and showing no signs of ever leaving. Also, Gen. Babangida was forced to leave office for an Interim Government as a result of the robust resistance of the civil society to his hidden agenda. For the period covered by this study only the Mohammed/Obasanjo regime could conceivably fit into Dare's typology of a 'reactive intervener' or what Amos Perlmutter refers to as the 'arbitrator type' regime. Others began as 'reactive interveners' but attempted to change to ' designed interveners'[37] or the 'ruler' type military regimes. For the purpose of clarity, Perlmutter distinguished between the 'arbitrator' type and the 'ruler' type military regimes as follows: The 'arbitrator type' "tends to be more professionally oriented ... (it) imposes a time limit on army rule and arranges to hand the government over to an 'acceptable' civilian regime." Whereas, 'the ruler type' regime deliberately develops "an independent political organisation and a fairly coherent and elaborate politi-

cal ideology" without entertaining the thoughts of returning to the barracks[38]. No matter the overt inclinations of the various military regimes under examination in this study, they were all compelled to disengage as at the time they did.

This brings to mind Dare's assertion that "the ability of any military regime to remain faithful to and carry out its pledge to disengage is directly related to the relative influence and pressure of the various interests and clienteles"[39]. He came to this conclusion after drawing attention to the problem of disengagement which he later broke down as follows:

(a) The fear about the nature of a succeeding regime

(b) The fear about personal safety after the transition

(c) The fear of policy reversal

(d) The fear that military privileges may be curtailed by the successor

(e) The fear of political deadlock after disengagement

(f) The belief that the developmental momentum may not be sustained by the successor regime.

(g) The belief that civilians are inherently poor administrators[40].

Thus, "(if) a regime is favourably disposed to staying, it can always find plausible rationalisations for that decision"[41]. This can range from the so-called ineptitude of the politicians to the need for more time to achieve certain objectives. In this devious way, Military disengagement or transition to civil rule programme could become a strategy for elongating military regimes. In fact this was the case under Gowon and Babangida regimes.

A significant feature of the disengagement exercise in Nigeria was the putting together of transition programmes intended to ease the military out of government and bring in the civilians. In essence, the term 'transition' "signifies the passage from one state to another ... It implies a break and a movement in another direction"[42]. It could take the form of violence as symbolised in civil war and coup d'etat or a peaceful type in which goals are expressly stated and methodically pursued through a well laid

out programme of action. This implies a process of careful selection and subsequent ordering of values and goals. Hence the implementation of a transition programme represents "a deliberate and conscious social engineering attempt by policy makers to move the society in alternative but positive direction"[43]. At least, this represents the ideal. But the reality of the situation in Nigeria was that for some of the regimes (Gowon's and Babangida's especially) transition was a ruse for perpetuating their rule in a disguised form. This was done by creating the impression that the civilian politicians were ill-prepared to shoulder the responsibilities of statecraft. Therefore, the military would have to continue to rule until such a time that the civilians would have learnt their lessons.

Anthony Kirk-Greene and Douglas Rimmer's *Nigeria Since 1970: A Political and Economic Outline*, offer some insights into the disengagement programmes of the military. Part One of the book, titled, "The Making of the Second Republic" is particularly rich in the treatment of the botched transition programme of the Gowon regime. They attempted to rationalise Gowon's *volte face* by suggesting that he was most probably alarmed by the violent reaction to the outcome of the census exercise he carried out in 1973. And, as a result, his regime could not handover in chaos. Yet some advisers had cautioned that as men of honour the military should not renege on its promise to handover to civilians on the appointed date no matter the situation at hand[44].The authors presented the picture of Gen. Gowon torn between two options. But as a result of his free-wheeling style of administration and "his willingness to listen to all comers and his appearing to accept the last point of view in his search for total agreement"[45,] he made a patriotic but unpopular choice as it turned out later. The above rationalisation would have been convincing if Gowon had faithfully implemented its Nine-Point transition programme from the very beginning. The controversial census which provided the excuse for scuttling the whole programme was number seven in the nine-point programme. Before it, the other items were either untouched or half-heartedly attended to.

In other words, four years into the six-year programme only the census exercise could be said to have been concluded before the fateful announcement on 1ˢᵗ October 1974 that the target date of 1ˢᵗ October 1976 was no longer realistic. A highly respected scholar, who did a thorough evaluation of the Gowon's transition programme, concluded rightly that the abandonment of the programme led to frustration and political disillusioment "not so much from the statement that 1976 was no longer realistic as from the fact that no alternative date was proposed. Gowon had simply said he would rule indefinitely"[46]. This cast doubts on Gowon's sincerity about and commitment to the transition programme. And, it also foreshadowed the now familiar military ploy of invoking spurious excuses to perpetuate its hold on political power.

Oyeleye Oyediran's edited work, *Nigerian Government and Politics Under Military Rule, 1966-1979*[47] shed more light on the military's disengagement programmes. Not only are the transition programmes clearly highlighted and the informing sensibilities discussed, there are also multi-dimensional scholarly analyses of the implementation strategies of the military actors. However, none of the contributors perceived transition as a covert strategy for power control. The experience of the Gowon period ought to have made this obvious. But, two of them, Bayo Adekanye (Adekson) and Oyeleye Oyediran, in a prognostic assessment of Nigeria's political future, agreed that the military might disengage physically but they raised the problem of the lure of office as the stumbling block in the way of psychological withdrawal[48]. These eminent scholars have been proved right by the recurring nature of coups and counter-coups in Nigeria.

Another important text on this subject is Billy Dudley's, *An Introduction to Nigerian Government and Politics*. It contained more indepth analysis of Nigeria's socio-economic environment as an important back drop to the prospect of the emergence of a truly democratic set up. Dudley devoted considerable space to the treatment of what he called 'The Political Economy of Military Rule'. Here he highlighted and discussed the corrupt practices,

economic mismanagement and the neglect of the masses under the military between 1966 and 1979.

He argued that,

> military rule and the oil boom could be said to have fostered the growth and spread of what might best be described as "commercial capitalism", enabling the military hierarchy and their civilian aides – the top bureaucrats, a few university men and the indigenous mercantilists – to emerge as the new dominant property –owning 'class' in the society[49].

Falola and Ihonvbere examined the influence of the 'new class' referred to by Dudley and observed that the political institutions (like the Constitution Drafting Committee – CDC and the Constituent Assembly – CA) established for the transition exercise were dominated by its members. Not only this, they also observed that the prohibitive cost stipulated by the Federal Electoral Commission (FEDECO) for the registration of political parties effectively screened-off the masses and workers. Thus, it is their contention that the disastrous outcome of the democratic experiment of the Second Republic had its roots in the deformed transition programme put in place by the Obasanjo regime. The massive rigging of the 1979 elections with the connivance of FEDECO[50] and the controversial interpretation of two-thirds of nineteen states to mean twelve two-thirds (as suggested by the legal adviser of one of the political parties)[51] in the determination of the presidential election bastardised the electoral process by formalising underhand tricks.

General Olusegun Obasanjo in his book, Not My Will, attempted to exculpate his administration from the poor performance of some of the institutions it established for the transition programme by asserting that the institutions (e.g. C.A. and FEDECO) were given a freehand to operate without interference from government [52]. His explanations on the controversial issue of 'twelve two-thirds' would have been convincing but for the fact that on the eve of his departure from office the electoral provision was reinterpreted to mean thirteen states and the con-

stitution was unilaterally amended to reflect this. Obasanjo also devoted a lot of space to show how he had literally bent backwards on a number of occasions to 'whitewash' Chief Awolowo's political image as a way of ensuring his (Awo's) 'national acceptance' and how such gestures were not appreciated by Awo. Private and official correspondence between Awo and himself and some "corroborative evidence"from other actors in the "Obasanjo-Awolowo"saga were referred to in order to prove Awolowo's intransigence[53].

Ebenezer Babatope in the book, *Not His Will: The Awolowo-Obasanjo Wager*, provide a fitting response to Obasanjo's claims. Here the issue of 'twelve two-thirds' was elaborately addressed[54] and the reputation of late Chief Awolowo was stoically defended. Babatope also exploded the myth of Obasanjo's self-proclaimed neutrality by observing that Gen. Obasanjo voted for Alhaji Shehu Shagari in the presidential elections. And that, "(if) indeed, contest at an election is based on the political computation of numbers, then a little administrative manipulation and subtle law got Shagari elected as President by mathematics"[55]. The point that is being underscored here is that when the military was compelled to transfer power to civilians in 1979 it preferred to be succeeded by a regime that would not only give it 'covering fire' but also ensure policy continuity. Obviously the staid and easy going Shagari was preferred to the 'puritanic' Awolowo who was rumoured to be threatening to probe the activities of the departing military rulers. Thus, far from being a neutral umpire the military actually manipulated the transition process to its advantage. This brings to mind Gavin Williams' observation on the 1979 transition exercise. He compared the exercise with the constitutional decolonisation by the British and affirmed that "(like) the British, the military government controlled effective political power and used it to direct constitutional discussions towards the outcome they preferred"[56].

From the above discourses it is apparent that the Second Republic suffered serious congenital problems which were not

unconnected with the undemocratic nature of the transition programme that gave birth to it. These can be summarised as:

(i) The vested interest of the incumbent military regime in determining who succeeds it.

(ii) The manipulation of the electoral and juridical processes to achieve this end.

(iii) The inability of the Obasanjo regime to effect a reorientation of attitudes towards public office.

Thus the Shagari administration which the transition programme produced was characterised by corruption, economic mismanagement and underhand political gimmicks. The situation came to a head in 1983 when it employed the resources at its disposal to manipulate the electoral process in order to remain in office. The crises and widespread disillusionment generated by this development provided the excuse for a military coup which brought Gen. Mohammed Buhari to power on the 31st of December 1983. This was a 'designed intervener' or a 'ruler type' military oligarchy and this was probably responsible for its short lifespan. Nigerians, as we have noted previously from Dare, Kirk-Greene and Rimmer, would not gladly tolerate a sit-tight military regime. The regime's sadistic and hardline disposition did not help matters either. This was all that was needed by an overly ambitious and power-hungry soldier like Gen. Ibrahim Babangida to stage a coup. Babangida rightly perceived the mood of the nation by promising a quick return to democratic governance, as soon as he took over.

General Babangida's perception of what a transition to democratic governance should entail and how this can be achieved are contained in the two volumes of his selected speeches put together by Olatunji Olagunju and Sam. Oyovbaire. In the first volume titled, *Portrait of a New Nigeria: Selected Speeches of IBB*, the first section opened with his maiden address to the nation in which he justified the change of government and exhorted Nigerians to be committed "to the course of building a strong, united and viable nation"[57]. Other sections in which the thinking of the government on a new political order for Nigeria are made

known include; "The Search for a New Political Order," "The Design of a New Constitution", "The March to a Viable Political Order," "Let us Learn From History," "The Making of the Third Republic", and "Reflections on a Political Programme for the Country"[58]. These were speeches delivered at various occasions in which institutions and bodies intended to facilitate the emergence of the new political order were inaugurated.

The informing sensibility in the drafting of the transition programme to the envisaged new political order as evident from some of the speeches is the belief that previous democratic transition programmes were hastily put together and hurriedly executed. Therefore the Babangida regime favoured a gradualistic approach which saw the democratic process as essentially a learning process that would be amenable to changes as it progresses. Babangida's address to the nation at the launching of the Transition to Civil Rule Programme on 1st July 1987 subscribed to this view. After carefully highlighting the content of the programme up to the period of the proposed military disengagement in 1992, he remarked that, "(as) you can see from the political programme it is aimed at establishing a gradual and graduated learning political culture"[59]. This prepared the ground for the virtually interminable transition under Babangida.

The second volume titled, *For Their Tomorrow We Gave Our Today: Selected Speeches of IBB Vol. II,* is essentially complementary to the first volume. However, this one is more directly related to the mechanics of evolving the new political order and the correlation between a vibrant political system and a healthy economy. First, the forceful imposition of the government sponsored two political parties on the transition programme was rationalized. This was done ostensibly to prevent 'money bags' from hijacking the parties[60].

Second, the role of policy-generating and facilitating agencies like the Mass Mobilisation for Social Justice and Economic Recovery (MAMSER), National Electoral Commission (NEC), Administrative Staff College of Nigeria (ASCON) and National Institute of Policy and Strategic Studies (NIPSS) were given

considerable attention[61]. Third, and most important, is the recognition of the fact that no truly democratic arrangement can be
evolved and sustained without a bouyant economy and socially
well placed citizenry. Section B, titled: "Economic Reforms
and the Development Imperative" is devoted to speeches on
economic reconstruction, policy initiative (e.g. SAP) and the
operations of facilitating agencies like the Technical Committee on Privatisation and Commercialisation (TCPC), National
Economic Recovery Fund (NERFUND), Peoples' Bank (PB)
etc. The policy options and the agencies were intended to effect
a positive reorientation of the economy to the benefit of all and
sundry or so it seemed. But the way and manner in which the
economic policies were executed left much to be desired. In particular the excruciating impact of SAP further worsened the lot
of the people[62]. The palliative measures initiated were too superficial and restrictive to strengthen the people. The result was a
pauperised and humbled citizenry who could not confront the
oppressive federal military government.

Tunji Olagunju, Adele Jinadu and Sam. Oyovbaire attempted
to throw more light on Babangida's transition programme in
Transition to Democracy in Nigeria (1985-1993). This book
written by 'participant observers'[63] in the transition programme
was obviously intended to:

(i) account for the role and level of involvement of the authors
     in the whole process, and,

(ii) to celebrate a *fait accompli* in the belief that the book's publi-
     cation would coincide with the successful conclusion of the
     transition.

Thus, the book is heavily-laden with eulogies of Babangida's
exploits. It was even dedicated to him. Obviously the authors
never reckoned with Babangida's hidden agenda which manifested in the unwarranted annulment of the presidential elections
that would have concluded the programme. Thus, at first reading
the book could be dismissed as a mere hagiography. But a closer
perusal shows that it has certain things worth highlighting.

First, the background details and behind the scene consultations that went into the drawing up of the transition programme were highlighted and discussed. From these it could be seen that a lot of thorough intellectual preparations preceded and informed the formulation of the programme[64]. Without doubt this would have conveyed the impression of commitment and sincerity on the part of the sponsor of the programme.

Second, the implementation strategies and the performance of the regime on the job were appraised. But a mistaken impression was created that Babangida's efforts were achieving fruitful results for the polity in spite of the misconduct of the civilian politicians[65]. It is important to note that certain actions of the Babangida administration (which the authors either ignored or glossed over) created a disenabling atmosphere for the nurturing of democracy and a smooth transfer of power. Such actions would include, the repudiation of the peoples' will by doctoring the report of the political bureau; the anti-democratic environment created through the imposition of SAP and its sustenance through coercive and repressive measures; the frequent arrest and incarceration of human rights and pro-democracy activists; the gagging of the press and the government tacit support and encouragement of pro-military and anti-democratic bodies, like Association for Better Nigeria (ABN), Third Eye and League of Patriots. No enduring democratic arrangement can ever emerge under this stifling and uncertain atmosphere. The authors observations were biased probably because of their direct involvement in the exercise which they wrote about. This raises the question of objectivity in writings done by participant observers[66].

Furthermore, the authors' adulation of their mentor (i.e. Babangida) prevented a proper evaluation of the effect of the regime's socio-economic and political programmes on the people who were at the receiving end. More balanced analysis of the implementation of Babangida's transition agenda have been put together by Bayo Adekanye[67] and Adeolu Akande[68]. Writing differently they reached similar conclusions which affirmed that Babangida merely used 'transition' as a strategy for extended

political power control before the people got wise to his antics and compelled him to relinquish power. This illustrates the truism in Chinua Achebe's observation that "(Power) does not only entice, intimidate and subdue; it may also incite to resentment and rebellion"[69].

CONCLUDING REMARKS

We have established, through the literature, that the military institution is rigid, authoritarian (or anti-democratic) and thrives on violence. This orientation was carried into politics and governance. It capitalised on its monopoly of the instruments of coercion and the ineptitude of civilian politicians to push itself into political reckoning. The 'corrective regime' claim has been the pretentious platform on which the military usually rationalises its disruption of the political process and the subsequent militarisation of the social polity. But the reality of the situation is that the spoils of office and the lust for power (in a manner reminiscent of Machiavelli's prescriptions) have been mostly responsible for military rule and the reluctance to disengage from politics.

In order to endear themselves to influential people in the polity and thereby secure popular acceptance, most military regimes were consciously patrimonial. The Babangida regime especially added a personalist touch which made him to loom larger than the military and the state in his heydays. His 'carrot and stick' style of administration and the devious manipulation of the internal political environment through an intricate network of patron-client connections singled out his regime as the hallmark of military political excesses in Nigeria.

It is paradoxical that the military rulers were laying claim to the ability to facilitate transition to democratic governance in spite of their antecedents and proclivities. In fact, this was a ruse for the only time that this was done it only served as a short term expediency during which the incompetence of the civilian politicians was exposed to the generality of the people. This then prepared the ground for the comeback of the 'corrective' military in a more formidable manner.

It is our belief that the military's corrective regime posturing, its coercive and repressive disposition leading to the militarisation of the polity, the politics of patronage and subordination, and the deformed or manipulated transition programmes were deliberate strategies to ensure and sustain military political dominance. Some of these strategies have been addressed by some authors as we have established, but chiefly under a particular regime (the Babangida regime). Our present effort is geared towards establishing the use to which these strategies were put by all the regimes that fall within the scope of our study. This is informed by the conviction that, fundamentally there was continuity under military dispensations in Nigeria while at the superficial level there were changes under the different regimes.

The focus of our study is the period 1966-1993. 1966 marked the beginning of military incursion into politics and 1993 the termination of the infamous Babangida era. The choice of this time frame affords us the opportunity of establishing the circumstances of military incursion into politics, the incidence of the civil war and how it enhanced military dominance, and the survival strategies that sustained the military in power.

The terminal date of 1993 chosen for the study is considered appropriate for us to make some definitive remarks about the military and the Nigerian state having observed the trend of events for more than a quarter of a century and based especially on our bizarre experience under the Gen. Babangida regime.

The attempt to gather information through oral interview met with limited success as only two retired army officers responded favourably. The other officers approached (both serving and retired) either preferred anonymity or declined outrightly. Given the size of the target population the number of respondents was considered to be too small. Therefore oral interview was jettisoned.

Thus we relied on archival materials, findings and documents from research institutes, private and government publications, periodicals, News Magazines and secondary materials broadly

relevant to the subject matter. A descriptive analytical method was employed in the study.

As a result of the continuity of some socio-political phenomena under different military dispensations and the need to avoid repetitions, a thematic (rather than narrative) approach is favoured for this study.

Apart from the introduction and conclusion, the study is divided into five chapters, four of which encapsulate the strategies frequently employed by military rulers to control power.

Chapter One titled: "Nature and Character of the Nigerian State and its Military Establishment before 1966", provides the necessary background to the study. In chapter Two the Military's incursion into politics is discussed and its 'corrective regime' claim is critically examined. Chapter Three deals with the politics of patronage and subordination while chapter four focuses on the deliberate militarisation of the Nigerian polity. The fifth chapter looks at 'Transition' as a strategy of power control.

Notes

1. J.Bayo Adekanye: "Military Organisation and Federal Society", in *Quarterly Journal of Administration* , XVI (I & 2). 1981/82. pp. 3-23.
2. Claude Ake: "The Significance of Military Rule", in *Proceedings of the National Conference on the Stability of the Third Republic* (Lagos: Concord Group, 1988) pp. 118-130.
3. Adekanye : Military Organisation ... p.3.
4. Ake : The Significance of Military Rule ... p. 120.
5. Ibid.
6. Kunle Amuwo: "The Return of the Military: A Theoretical Construct and Explanation", in Adejumobi, S. and Momoh A. (eds): *The Political Economy of Nigeria Under Military Rule* (Harare: SAPES Books, 1995) p.3.
7. J. Bayo Adekanye : "The Military in the Transition", in Larry Diamond A. Kirk-Greene and Oyeleye Oyediran (eds): *Transition Without End: Nigerian Politics and Civil Society Under Babangida*, (Ibadan: Vantage Publishers, 1997) p.56.

8. D.C. Rapopport: "A Comparative Theory of Military and Political Types", in Huntington, S.P. (ed.) *Changing Patterns of Military Politics* (New York: Free Press, 1962) p. 78.

9. M.D. Feld: *The Structure of Violence: Armed Forces and Social Systems* (Beverly Hills: SAGE Publications, 1977) p.32.

10. B.J. Dudley: "The Military and Politics in Nigeria", in Van Doorn (ed.): *Military Profession and Military Regimes* (The Hague: Mouton & Co. Publishers, 1969) p.208.

11. Amuwo : *The Return of the Military* ... p. 3.

12. Toyin Falola and Julius Ihonvbere: *The Rise and Fall of Nigeria's Second Republic, 1979-1984* (London: Zed Books Ltd., 1985) p. 240.

13. J. 'Bayo Adekanye: *Military Occupation and Social Stratification – An Inaugural Lecture* (Ibadan: Vantage Publishers (Int.) Ltd., 1993) pp. 4-5.

14. Kunle Amuwo : "The Nigerian Military as a New Class", in Proceedings of the 16th Annual Conference of the Nigerian Political Science Association (NPSA) 1989, Section 7, p. 2.

15. Quoted in, Robert A. Dahl: 'Power', in *International Encyclopedia of the Social Sciences*, Vol. 11, p. 406.

16. Olufemi Taiwo: "Political Obligation and Military Rule", in *The Philosophical Forum* xxviii (2) Winter 1996, p. 170.

17. Quoted in *Ibid*, pp. 170-171

18. *Ibid.*, p. 171.

19. See, J.Bayo Adekanye: "Machiavelli and the Military: The Prince and the Psychology of Empty Power", in *Strategic Studies* (Islamabad) III(2) 1985, pp. 9-36 and "The Military in the Transition" in Larry Diamond *et al* (eds.): *Transition Without End* ... pp. 55-80.

20. Adekanye: The Military ... p. 72.

21. A.O.Akande: "Machiavellian Statecraft; Corporatism and Neopatrimonial Rule: Nigeria Under General Babangida", Unpublished Ph.D. Thesis, University of Ibadan, Ibadan, 1997.

22. Adekanye: The Military ... p. 72.

23. Eboe Hutchful: "Military Issues in the Transition to Democracy", in Eboe Hutchful and Abdoulaye Bathily (eds.): *The Military and Militarism in Africa*, (Dakar: CODESRIA, 1998) pp. 604-605.

24. Amos Perlmutter: "The Praetorian State and the Praetorian Army," in *World Politics* 1(3) April 1969, Pp 382-385.

25. S. Adejumobi: "The Military as Economic Manager: The Babangida Regime and the Structural Adjustment Programme", Unpublished Ph.D. Thesis, University of Ibadan, Ibadan, 1999, p. 32.

26. Akande: Machiavellian Statecraft ... p. 74.

27. Rene Lemarchand and Keith Legg: "Political Clientelism and Development: A Preliminary Analysis", in *Comparative Politics* 4(2) 1972, p. 15.

28. James C. Scott: "Patron-Client Politics and Political Change in South East Asia", in *American Political Science Review* 61(1) 1972, p. 92.

29. Peter Flynn: "Class, Clientelism and Coercion: Some Mechanisms of Internal Dependency and Control", in *Journal of Commonwealth and Comparable Studies,* 22(1), 1980 p. 134.

30. Lemarchand and Legg: Political Clientelism ... p. 15.

31. Richard Sandbrook: "Patrons, Clients and Factions: New Dimensions of Conflict Analysis in Africa", in *Canadian Journal of Political Science* 5(1) 1972, p. 119.

32. Richard Sandbrook : *The Politics of African Economic Stagnation,* (Cambridge: Cambridge University Press, 1983). p.83.

33. See below, Chapter Three.

34. L.O. Dare: *The Praetorian Trap: The Problems and Prospects of Military Disengagement* – Inaugural Lecture, Obafemi Awolowo University, Ile-Ife, 1991, p. 17.

35. A Kirk-Greene and D. Rimmer: *Nigeria Since 1970: A Political and Economic Outline* (London: Hodder and Stoughton, 1981) p. 54.

36. Dare: The Praetorian Trap ... pp. 17-18.

37. Ibid., p. 17

38. Amos Perlmutter: The Praetorian State ... pp. 382-383.

39. L. Dare: "Military Withdrawal From Politics in Nigeria", in *International Political Science Review* 3, 1981, pp. 51-62.

40. Dare: The Praetorian Trap ... pp. 15-16.

41. *Ibid.* p. 16.

42. Z.G. Feidinad and M. W. De Saiza: "Democratic Transition and Good Governance In Africa: Methods of Sharing Positive Experiences Among African Countries", in A. Aderinwale (ed.): *Conclu-*

sions and Papers Presented at Conferences of the African Leadership Forum (Abeokuta: ALF, 1993) p. 27.

43. See, H. Nwosu: "The Transition Programme, Election and Political Stability in Nigeria" – Lecture delivered at the 11th Congress of the Students' Historical Society of Nigeria, Ibadan, 21st May, 1991, p. 1.
44. Kirk-Greene and Rimmer: Nigeria Since 1970 ... p. 7.
45. Ibid.
46. Billy J. Dudley: *An Introduction to Nigerian Government and Politics* (London: Macmillan Pub. Ltd., 1982) p. 82.
47. Oyeleye Oyediran (ed.): *Nigerian Government and Politics Under Military Rule, 1966-1979* (Lagos: Friends Foundations Publishers Limited, 1988).
48. See, J. 'Bayo Adekanye (Adekson): "Dilemma of Military Disengagement" and Oyeleye Oyediran: "Civilian Rule for How Long?", in *Ibid.* pp. 231 and 287 respectively.
49. Dudley: An Introduction ... p. 120.
50. For details, see, *Report of the Judicial Commission of Inquiry into the Affairs of the Federal Electoral Commission (FEDECO) 1979-1983* (Lagos: Federal Government Printer, 1991).
51. It will be recalled that Chief Richard Akinjide of the National Party of Nigeria (NPN) first interpreted the electoral law to mean twelve two-thirds states in a television programme.
52. Olusegun Obasanjo: *Not My Will,* (Ibadan: University Press Ltd., 1990) p. 172.
53. Ibid. pp. 198-202.
54. Ebenezer Babatope: *Not His Will: The Awolowo-Obasanjo Wager,* (Benin City: Jodah Publications, 1990) pp. 1-44.
55. *Ibid.* p. 44.
56. Gavin Williams: *State and Society in Nigeria* (Idanre: Afrografika Publishers, 1980) p. 15.
57. Olatunji Olagunju and Sam Oyovbaire (ed.): *Portrait of a New Nigeria: Selected Speeches of IBB* (Lagos: Precision Press, not dated) p. 26.
58. Ibid. p. 27- 96.
59. Ibid. p. 94

60. See O. Olagunju and S. Oyovbaire (eds.): *For Their Tomorrow We Gave Our Today: Selected Speeches of IBB, Vol. II* (Ibadan: Safari Books Ltd., 1991) pp. 1-43.

61. Ibid. p. 71.

62. For a discourse, see, S. Adejumobi: The Military as Economic Managers ...

63. It will be recalled that Professor Sam. Oyovbaire was a member of the Political Bureau. Later, he and Dr. Olagunju were ministers in the Transition Council. Professor Adele Jinadu was a political adviser to the regime.

64. Tunji Olagunju, Adele Jinadu and Sam. Oyovbaire: *Transition to Democracy in Nigeria, 1985-1993* (Ibadan: Safari Books Ltd., 1993) pp. 25-195.

65. *Ibid.* pp. 245-254.

66. For a discourse, see, E.H. Carr: *What is History?* (Middlesex: Penguin Books, 1964) pp. 119-123.

67. Adekanye: "The Military",in Larry Diamond *et al* (eds.):Transition Without End ... pp.55-80.

68. Akande: Machiavellian Statecraft ...

69. Chinua Achebe: *The Trouble With Nigeria* (Enugu: Fourth Dimension Pub. Company Ltd., 1983) p. 31.

NATURE AND CHARACTER OF THE NIGERIAN STATE AND ITS MILITARY ESTABLISHMENT BEFORE 1966

THE PRE-COLONIAL AND COLONIAL ANTECEDENTS

Nigeria is situated along the West Coast of Africa with a coastline that stretches for about 800 kilometres from Badagry in the west to Calabar in the East, including the Bights of Benin and Bonny. It has an area of 570,000 square kilometres, (365,669 square miles)[1] sharing borders with the Republic of Benin to the West, Niger Republic to the North and the Republic of Cameroon to the East. According to the 1963 census returns (which has remained the reference point for all times)[2] it has a population of 55,671,000. It consists of many ethnic groups speaking diverse languages and having different socio-cultural traits and ways of life. Notable examples are the Kanuri, Hausa, Yoruba, Tiv, Jukun, Edo, Igbo, Efik, Ibibio, Urhobo, Itsekiri and Ijo.

These ethnic groups had been organised into various autonomous empires, kingdoms and states of varying sizes with advanced systems of government. These states and kingdoms jealously guarded their independence. Although some of these political entities sometimes exerted influence (through wars and commercial intercourse) on territories outside their natural confines, such influences were either superficial and/or transient. There was no political arrangement incorporating the various groups before the colonial period.

The diverse groups were forcefully brought together as a British colony under foreign juridiction Act of 1890. The Act stipulates, amongst other things, that,

> It shall be lawful for His Majesty the king to hold, exercise, and enjoy any jurisdiction which His Majesty now has or may at any time hereafter have within a foreign country in the same and as ample a manner as if His Majesty had acquired that Jurisdiction by the cession or conquest of Teritory[3].

This was an imposition as the feelings of the affected peoples were not taken into consideration.

As a matter of fact many peoples and communities of the colonial territory were not parties to the defining of the territory and relationships which they were compelled to sustain during the period of colonial rule and thereafter. Karl Deutsch captured the essence of our discussion succinctly in the following words: "(More) often they (the colonial territories -ours) have inherited boundaries drawn for administrative or political convenience by foreign colonial rulers, as in the cases of India, Pakistan, Argentina, Nigeria and Ghana"[4]. As L.O. Dare has rightly stated, "(being) multi-ethnic or plural societies, their primordial attachment to ethnicity is far stronger than to the new national entity"[5].

The colonial territories around the River Niger (later named Nigeria) were initially divided into three protectorates under separate administrations. These were the Lagos, Southern and Northern protectorates. The process of the unification of the protectorates into one entity started in 1906 when the Lagos and Southern protectorates were amalgamated. This was followed in 1914 by the amalgamation of the 'new' southern protectorate and the Northern protectorate to form the Protectorate of Nigeria.

The preamble to the Nigerian Protectorate Order in Council 1913 states unequivocally that "it is expedient that the Protectorates of Northern Nigeria and Southern Nigeria shall be formed into one protectorate under the name of the protectorate of Nigeria"[6]. Administrative convenience, economic and fiscal necessities made the move expedient and desirable for the colonial master. It was therefore not considered important that

the subjects should be consulted. To this extent, Nigeria was an 'artificial' British creation[7].

Unfortunately the colonial policy of 'divide and rule' did not allow the artificial unity to mature into a wholesome arrangement before independence was granted. Although under the Clifford Constitution of 1922 a Legislative Council was established for the first time for the whole nation, its jurisdiction was restricted to the southern provinces. In other words it could not legislate for the Northern province[8]. Also there was an Executive Council for the Nation but this was made up entirely of British officials who were only responsible to the Governor[9]. It was not until 1st January 1947 when the Richards' Constitution of 1946 came into effect that the Northern provinces were effectively brought within the legislative competence of the newly established Nigerian Legislative Council[10].

The same Richards' constitution, however, introduced Regional Houses of Assembly and Regional governments into the country[11]. For this purpose the country was split into three regions: North, West and East. This move enfeebled the fledgling national liberation movement by encouraging separatist tendencies. Before now the National Council of Nigeria and the Cameroons (NCNC) had existed (since August 1944) as the first political organisation with a clear-cut political ideology for the decolonisation of Nigeria[12]. But with the introduction of the Richards' constitution the nationalist trend was adversely affected. Dr. Nnamdi Azikiwe, the foremost nationalist leader, captured the situation appropriately when he described the constitution as a design to "Pakistanise" the country and "to departmentalise the political thinking of Nigerians"[13]. In 1947, Azikiwe led the NCNC in a nationwide tour to educate the people on the fissiparous tendencies of the constitution. This was the first attempt to bring national politics to the people at the grass root level and the attempt was fairly successful.

The unpopularity of the new constitutional arrangement as depicted by the reactions to it within the country necessitated the recall of Governor Richards. He was replaced by Sir John

Macpherson. In 1950, the All-Nigeria Constitutional Conference (which was intended to break the ground for the introduction of a new constitution as promised by Macpherson) was convened at Ibadan. It will be recalled that one of the major criticisms levelled against the Richards' constitution was that it was imposed on Nigerians. Macpherson, therefore, gave the impression of responding to the wishes of the people by convening the Ibadan conference. But the way and manner in which the conference was constituted left much to be desired[14]. A Nigerian scholar who did a thorough evaluation of the composition of this conference has concluded rightly that the unwieldy system employed in nominating members for the conference was a deliberate British strategy which would ensure that it was dominated by conservative elements who would endorse British design to emasculate the country and thereby ensure perpetual dependence[15].

The way and manner in which issues of national importance were handled and resolved at the conference lends credence to this view. For instance, on the issue of whether Nigeria should have a strong centre or a Federal arrangement with considerable autonomy for the regions, the Northern conservatives (as a result of the size and population of their region) not only wanted the status quo to remain but they also demanded half the seats in the House of Representatives. They also insisted that revenue allocation should be based on per capita distribution rather than on the principle of derivation. Quite expectedly the southerners kicked against this move seeing it as an attempt to impose Northern hegemony on the country. This notwithstanding, the British, in their attempt to conciliate the Northerners and thereby control the country behind the scenes, proceeded to introduce a constitution (Macpherson constitution) in which the Central Legislature was to comprise 148 members. Of this number, 136 were to be Nigerians with 68 members from the Northern House and 34 each from the Eastern and Western Houses of Assembly[16]. Thus, the constitution further endorsed the federal arrangement put forward by the Richards' constitution.

The conservative elements in the country saw in the new arrangement the opportunity to exercise power in their respective regions with minimum interference from the central government. Therefore, in order to contest the forthcoming elections within the provisions of the Macperson constitution, two regional parties were established. They were the Action Group (AG) in the West and the Northern Peoples Congress (NPC) in the North[17].

The outcome of the elections of 1951/52 effectively sealed any hope of a united front. Gabriel Olusanya simply states that, "the NPC won in the North, the A.G. in the West, and the NCNC in the East"[18]. However, it has been established that the NCNC won majority of the seats in the Western House of Assembly but as a result of political manouevring in which bribery was suspected, a number of NCNC candidates crossed the carpet to A.G's side[19].

Furthermore, the AG did not only refuse to recognise Azikiwe as the leader of opposition in the Western House of Assembly, but it also took advantage of the internal disorder in the NCNC to prevent him from being elected into the Central Legislature in 1952[20]. The A.G. attitude coupled with the pressure brought upon him by his Igbo supporters to come over to the East and rule (especially after the dissolution of the Eastern House of Assembly in 1953) made Azikiwe yield to the forces of reaction. The effect of this *volte face* (on the part of Zik) on nationalist struggle is vividly put across in the following statement by Professor Eni Njoku, a dissident NCNC member:

> How can they (the NCNC) really explain the fact that Zik now appears to accept self-government in instalments, regionalisation and pakistanisation?
>
> ... Awolowo has indeed achieved a great victory and captured Zik in the bargain
>
> ... And so ends the dream of One Country, One Destiny. And so even Zik, who aspired to be a national leader, is now content to be a tribal chief[21].

By his tactical withdrawal from the West, Zik now gave the AG the opportunity to further consolidate itself in the region and also to start assuming the role of a national party. For instance, the AG (without due consultation with other political parties) sponsored the motion for self-government in the House of Representatives in March 1953. Speaking on the motion, Anthony Enahoro, an AG member, urged the House "to accept as a primary political objective the attainment of self-government for Nigeria in 1956"[22]. The Northern elite for fear of southern domination opposed the motion. Ahmadu Bello, the NPC leader, argued that independence in 1956 would amount to political suicide and he proceeded to suggest the phrase, "as soon as practicable" to replace 1956 [23].

The colonialists capitalised on this situation of discordance and through the Lyttelton constitution of 1954 gave the regions more powers. Most importantly, the constitution promised self-government for any region that wanted it by 1956. This pleased the AG members and surprisingly Zik too, who hailed the move as an 'offer of self government on a platter of gold'. Predictably both the Western and Eastern Regions became self-governing by 1956 while the Northern region did not become self-governing until 1959. The most striking feature of Nigeria's nationalist struggle is that it did not produce a nationally accepted rallying figure. This in itself would not have posed a serious problem but for the fact that the emergent leaders were parochial, docile and conservative. They cleverly avoided a head-on collision with the colonial government in their struggles for emancipation because they did not want to rock the boat.

Nnamdi Azikiwe the leader of the anti-colonial movement in the 1940s was not a revolutionary and he detested violence[24]. Chief Obafemi Awolowo, the A. G. leader from the Western region, also shied away from violence. And, of course, the Northern oligarchy as represented by the Sardauna of Sokoto, Sir Ahmadu Bello, abhorred any confrontational attitude towards the colonisers[25]. In short, the leaders' attitudes manifested mainly in verbal tirades, newspaper articles, litigations and petitions,

except for occasional sporadic and unco-ordinated riots which occurred in Port Harcourt, Onitsha, Calabar and Aba in spontaneous reaction to the Enugu colliery shooting incident in 1949. In this shooting incident, twenty-nine persons were killed and fifty-one were wounded[26]. In fact, the 'Zikist Movement' that was said to have master-minded the riots was banned because it lacked the necessary backing of Nnamdi Azikiwe, the man who inspired the young men into action. He was even said to have denigrated them as "fissiparous lieutenants and cantankerous followers"[27].

The colonial period was also utilised by the colonialists to tie the Nigerian economy to that of the metropolis through which it was integrated into the international capitalist system. Before the advent of the colonisers, traditional agricultural endeavours were geared primarily to catering for the needs of the various communities and the surpluses were exchanged in the inter-community trade. But with the coming of the colonial overlords, this pattern was disrupted and supplanted by a system which saw to the diversion of the economy towards production for the purpose of feeding the industries in the imperialist countries. For this purpose, new crops were either introduced or the production of existing ones was given more impetus. The important crops then were cocoa, groundnut, palm produce and cotton.

Consequently, there developed an economic pattern in which raw materials mainly in the form of 'cash crops' were taken from the colony to the metropolis for processing. The establishment of the Railway system and the construction of the rail lines through circuitous routes were intended to facilitate the collection of raw materials from the hinterland to the coastal cities for shipment abroad. There was no attempt to stimulate the development of local industries that could utilise these materials. Significantly during the decolonisation process the crusaders failed to effect a re-orientation of these stifling economic pattern. While some of them in their hurry to secure independence believed that with political independence all other problems would be solved; some did not see anything wrong in the colonial economic arrange-

ment. The general assumption was that they could master the situation after attaining independence. But as things turned out, it mastered them[28].

NIGERIA AT INDEPENDENCE: THE POLITICS OF THE FIRST REPUBLIC

> The end of the anti-colonial struggle was the beginning of politics – and what was politics if not tribalism? What else was there to argue about? Tribes were more sharply differentiated than social classes... Now that the British were gone, the main thing to argue about was how to share a severely limited national cake[29].

The statement above poignantly captured the essence of the politics of the First Republic in Nigeria. As we have established in the preceding section the political parties of that period had undisguised sectional roots and were in essence champions of ethnic interests. The political parties and their leaders were so determined to strengthen their bargaining positions at the centre that they ignored the norms and rules of electoral competition and resorted to zero-sum-game or winner-takes-all strategies. This orientation determined the nature and character of the politics of the First Republic. The all-pervading phenomenon of rising expectations, based on electoral promises, and which the parties wanted to meet in order to satisfy their constituencies, actually compounded the problem.

We can recall that contrary to expectation independence brought misery and disllusionment to the masses in Nigeria. It is worth recalling here that in the twilight days of colonial rule there was a groundswell of expectation premised on the belief that with independence all problems would be solved and life would become more abundant. Rapid transformation in developmental terms, social advancements in the area of education, health, employment and other welfare indicators were largely anticipated and eagerly awaited. Unfortunately, such expectations did not reckon with the 'alien' Nigerian state that emerged

at independence. The neo-colonial form and character of many emergent African states (Nigeria inclusive) and the self-seeking propulsion of the emergent leaders – euphemistically referred to by Davidson as 'pirates in power'[30] – made nonsense of such expectations. The situation described above did not give room for any fundamental welfarist orientation.

It is instructive to note that at independence the control of the important sectors of Nigeria's economy remained within the grip of foreign (mainly British) concerns. The heavily dependent agrarian economy was the first indication of a dependence syndrome. The import/export business and the internal distributive trade were also dominated by foreign firms like the United African Company (UAC), John Holt, Paterson and Zochonis (PZ) etc. In construction business there was Richard Costain and in the Oil sector, Shell-BP was in control. These foreign firms drained the economy through capital flight and other ruthless devices. The former colonial master and her capitalist allies, too, did their utmost to sustain this unhealthy relationship. They deliberately inundated the country with various forms of loans, aids and technical assistance. For instance, within the first two years of her independence the U.S. offered a staggering sum of $225m aid to Nigeria out of which $39m was in the form of grants[31]. Between 1961 and 1963 the number of U.S. technical personnel in Nigeria increased by more than 200 percent[32]. Between 1962 and 1965 Britain's share of the total foreign investment in Nigeria was 66.9%, 62.5%, 57.9% and 56% respectively[33].

It has also been established that in 1962, 70% of Nigerian imports came from Western Europe, the Commonwealth and the U.S., while 90% of her exports went to those countries[34]. All these ensured very strong economic bond. It should be noted also that the state was the principal actor while state officials were the greatest beneficiaries of the skewed economic arrangement. The pivotal role of the state in Nigeria's economy as depicted in its appropriation of national resources and products has been well established as a social reality. According to Ralph Miliband, "the state is here the source of economic power as well as an instru-

ment of it; the state is a major means of production"[35]. Terisa Turner, provides greater insight into the 'power' of the Nigerian state by affirming that, "state control stems mainly from its role as a major buyer, but also from its regulatory power over other commercial activities"[36]. The result is the evolution of a network of commercial relations built around the state.

The partners in this network have been identified as: the businessman representing the multi-national corporations; the local middleman from the national private sector; and the state official who facilitates access to the local market for the foreign businessman[37]. The network exhibits two distinct patterns. First, a foreign businessman who wants to sell his company's products or desires to win a contract hires a local citizen to assist in lobbying state officials. At the successful conclusion of the deal, the state official is rewarded by the middleman or go-between usually with a previously agreed upon payment. This is the triadic variant of the network. Second, there is also the pattern in which the state comprador deals directly with the representative(s) of the firm without going through a middleman[38]. This is the dyadic variant.

In both cases the state official is the most powerful link "since the state not only awards contracts, but it sets terms for the sale of oil, crops or for the establishment of a business"[39]. In other words, "the state controls opportunities to profit through commerce"[40]. Therefore "politics becomes dominated by struggles for positions in the state or for access to those who have influence over government decisions"[41]. Thus, rapacious intentions rather than fidelity and commitment to public service underlay the frequent acrimonious struggle for the control of the Nigerian state in the First Republic. This is to be expected because whoever or whichever group controls the state and its machineries would not only have an unrestricted access to stupendous wealth, but also to the much needed security and protection to enjoy the anticipated windfall.

It is hardly surprising therefore that the emergent ruling elite was unduely reliant on state resources for private accumulation. It was an extractive rather than a productive class. In fact,

it was content to act as agents or facilitators of the neo-colonial exploitative forces as long as her 'commissions' are assured. The prevalent attitude amongst the ruling elite was to sustain and even reinforce the colonial economic arrangement in which the economies of the colonies were deliberately orientated towards serving that of the metropolis. Every suggestion or move towards nationalisation of foreign investments and trade liberalisation was regularly rebuffed[42]. Instead, most of the politicians were more interested in scrambling for state offices which would put them in a position of advantage to draw maximum benefits from the state-centred neo-colonial economy.

Quite expectedly Nigerian politics in the First Republic was acrimonious and ruthlessly self seeking. Acts of thuggery, arson, election rigging and ethnic jingoism were regularly employed for political ascendancy and the control of the state. This kind of situation encouraged persistent conflicts amongst the political elite. The parochial activities of regionally-based political parties and their acrimonious struggle to control the centre also threatened to pull the nation apart many times before the military took over the reins of government in 1966. It is worth recalling that the 1959 Federal elections shot the Northern People's Congress (NPC) into prominence but its votes were not enough to form the independence government singlehandedly. It, therefore, went into coalition with the NCNC to form the national government. The AG formed the opposition in the parliamentary system of government that was adopted. The opposition was very zealous while the government was intolerant and unyielding[43].

The first indication of the unhealthy relations was the declaration of a state of emergency in the western region (the opposition's political base) by the Federal Government in 1962. The internal crisis within the AG, which manifested in the personality clashes among the party leaders, provided the excuse for the Federal intervention. As if this was not enough, in September 1963 notable leaders of the AG were jailed on charges of treason[44]. Before now there had been the census crisis of 1962 which was patched-up with another equally controversial exercise in 1963. The dis-

puted figures of this latest attempt were eventually adopted for the nation. It should be noted that census had become seriously politicised because of the crucial role which population plays in revenue allocation, constituency de-limitation and the allocation of seats in the parliament. Thus census returns were often manipulated for political reasons. While some influential ethnic groups may have their population inflated other less privileged ones could have theirs depressed. This development compounded the strained relationship amongst the ethnic groups.

The simmering discontent amongst the populace was cannalised into national agitation through the General Strike of 1964. This further put the precarious economy in jeopardy. Before the situation could be normalised there was the federal election crisis which spilled over to 1965. The incumbent government had employed all tricks to rig the election in order to remain in office. This cast aspersion on the integrity of the government. It was, however, the Western regional election crisis of 1965 and the role of the Federal Government in it that actually sounded the death knell of that civilian administration. It has been established that the NPC-controlled federal government was solidly behind the Nigerian National Democratic Party (NNDP) – a coalition party of a break-away faction of the AG and the NPC – in whose favour the election was blatantly rigged[45].

Furthermore, when the chaotic situation generated by the electoral crisis reached alarming proportions such that law and order had broken down completely[46] the federal government remained nonchalant. Apparently, it saw in the situation an opportunity to destabilise the opposition and thereby gain permanent political foothold in that region. But the lukewarm attitude of the federal government to the security and political fortunes of the Western region made it unpopular. In its desperate bid to remain in power at all cost the incumbent government was always using the military for what ordinarily should have been police duties. This had the unforeseen consequence of rehearsing the military for political duties.

According to Robin Luckham,

> (The) internal security operations in which the military was asked to play a part-most notably in pacifying the Tiv in 1960 and 1964, maintaining essential services during the 1964 general strike and policing the Western Region after the regional elections of October 1965 – made it clear to those soldiers who cared to think about it that the survival of the existing political order depended upon them[47].

Thus, the weakening in legitimacy of the civilian authorities during the first years of independence and the widespread disillusionment among the people created the context for military intervention. In fact, the situation degenerated to the extent that the option of a messiah that would rescue the ship of state was thrown up. In other words, a credibility gap was created and waiting to be filled by a more assertive (but not necessarily more progressive) social force. This was the socio-political background to the military incursion into Nigerian politics. As a necessary complement to the background established above there is also a need to examine briefly the historical development of the military establishment in order to ascertain its preparedness for the political role which it started to play as from 15th January 1966.

THE EVOLUTION AND POLITICISATION OF THE MILITARY

Historically the Nigerian Army (the oldest arm of the military and the core of its operations) is an offspring of the West African Frontier Force (WAFF)- a Constabulary Force later renamed the Royal West African Frontier Force (RWAFF). This was a colonial force made up of contingents of soldiers from the British West African colonies. As the name suggests, it was established to service colonial interests in the area of border patrols and ceremonial functions. Before the coming into being of the WAFF there were three local forces which had assisted the colonial master in clamping down on local opposition to British penetration. These were;

(i) the Lagos Constabulary (originally known as "Glover's Hausa' or "Hausa Militia') which carried out punitive expeditions against the Ijebus in 1892 and Oyo in 1895;

(ii) the Royal Niger Constabulary established in 1886 to safeguard the commercial interests of the Royal Niger Company (RNC). This Force was also responsible for the subjugation of Nupe and Ilorin in 1897. In 1900 it was incorporated into the Northern Nigeria Regiment; and,

(iii) the Niger Coast Constabulary, originally known as the 'Oil Rivers Irregulars' established in 1891 to safeguard British interests along the Niger Coast. It was responsible for the subjugation of Ebrohimi in 1894 and Benin in 1897.

These forces were incorporated as the Nigerian Regiment of the WAFF when it was formed in 1898.

In 1922, this arrangement was given legal backing through the West African Frontier Force (Nigerian Regiment) Ordinance[48]. In 1956 the body was renamed Nigerian Military Forces – Royal West African Frontier Force. At independence it became the Royal Nigerian Army and in 1963, when Nigeria became a Republic, it became the Nigerian Army[49].

The Navy had been established in 1958 in compliance with the Navy Act of 1956 while the Airforce was established later, in 1964, to make a full-fledged military organisation. From the historical background given above, it is very easy to see why the army has been the most prominent segment of the armed forces in Nigeria. In fact the other segments (Navy and Air Force) are merely supportive organs of the army – dominated military organisation. More importantly, the circumstances of its birth, its humble beginning and its limited praetorian orientation did not call for the recruitment of any special elite into the military. Little or no premium was placed on education in its early years. Ordinary martial qualities would do. Thus menfolk from certain ethnic group were favoured, in terms of recruitment, for their so-called courage and resilience. This could conceivably mark the beginning of the politicization of the military through recruitment.

The evolutionary process of the military as a social institution has serious implications for its nature and disposition in the post-colonial period. First, it should be appreciated that the institution was set up by a predatory colonial power to foster the establishment and sustenance of colonial rule and exploitation. Consequently it could not participate or lend support to the anti-colonial struggles. Miners put the situation in clearer perspective by asserting that,

> The Military forces in these territories had been created not to defend the inhabitants against foreign attack but to assist foreigners to conquer the country... they were certainly not national armies and they played no part in the struggle for independence[50].

Since the forces were alienated from the anti-colonial struggles they were not in a position to appreciate the political engineering process exemplified in dialogue, compromise, tolerance, conflicts and crises. These attributes were strange to an institution that was nurtured on an unquestioning obedience to superior authorities. Thus, the military was unable to forge a good working relationship or have respect for the political elite whom they were inclined to view as disorderly and cantankerous. In fact "politicians were perjoratively described as 'bloody civilians', who possibly could be supplanted when the need arises"[51]. Thus, the two groups marched towards independence with barely concealed mutual suspicion.

Second, there was also the fact of the dimunitive occupational status and the low esteem in which the society held the military. Adekanye has demonstrated, in a well researched study, how the military was poorly ranked in terms of occupational status in the newly independent Nigerian state. He affirmed that the low literacy level and the hardly perceptible contribution of the institution to national development were important factors for its lowly ratings[52]. Obviously the military was not comfortable with its unenviable position. It is to be expected therefore that any opportunity to change the situation for the better would be eagerly seized and maximised. Although, Adejumobi has argued

that "this (i.e. the military's desire to change its status) may not appear as a reason for the seizure of political power by the institution"[53] ,the fact remains, as he (Adejumobi) later conceded, that "the rise of military rule in Nigeria is associated with the sudden rise in the social status, pay and general remuneration of the institution"[54]. This should not come as a surprise given our earlier observation that the control of the state in Nigeria would literally translate to 'hitting a goldmine' because of the diverse opportunities for the appropriation of national resources for self or reference groups.

Third, the nascent military institution was neither cohesive (as it appeared on the surface) nor detribalised. We can recall that in 1958 the quota system of recruitment into the military was formalised. Under this arrangement 50% of the available places were reserved for the Northern region, 25% each for the Eastern and Western regions. Even when the Mid-West was carved out of the Western region the quota allotted to the North and East remained while the West had to relinquish 4% of its quota to the new region. This development marked a watershed in the politicization of the military in Nigeria[55]. As Bayo Adekanye has rightly argued, "quota as a basis of recruitment is a political, rather than military, criterion". Therefore, "quota could not but have infected with its politics the Nigerian military which employed it"[56].

Hence the military organisation that emerged at independence was neither revolutionary nor immuned from tribal politics. On the surface it appeared neutral and apolitical, but fundamentally it had been conditioned, as from its early days, to enforce dominant class interests. In other words it has been functioning as the coercive wing of the ruling class. Although it was not directly involved in politics and politicking, its exposure to matters that had strong socio-political significance like the quota system of recruitment and the quelling of civil disturbances, politicised the military in Nigeria. By January 1966 it had waxed strong enough to assume a political role for itself.

Notes

1. See Margaret Peil, *Nigerian Politics: The People's View*, London: Cassel & Company Ltd., 1976 pp. 7-8.

2. The census figures of 1971 and 1991 were considered incredible and so unacceptable to the vast majority of the people. And so the government has been falling back on the 1963 returns and projecting therefrom for the purpose of planning and development.

3. Cited in, Nigerian Protectorate Order in Council, 1913 (preamble).

4. Karl Deutch: *Politics and Government*, 2nd ed. New York: Houghton Mifflin Company, 1974, p. 55

5. L.O.Dare: "The Praetorian Trap: The Problems and Prospects of Military Disengagement – Inaugural Lecture Series 94, Ile-Ife; OAU Press, Ltd., 1989, p. 8.

6. Nigerian Protectorate Order in Council, 1913 p. 1

7. For more details, see T.N. Tamuno: *The Evolution of Nigerian State: The Southern Phase, 1898-1914*, Ibadan: Longman, 1978. pp. 233-245.

8. B.O. Nwabueze: *A Constitutional History of Nigeria* (London; Longman Group Ltd, 1982.

9. *Ibid.*, p. 41.

10. *Ibid.*, p. 42.

11. *Ibid.*, p. 127.

12. At its first constitutional conference in January 1947 the NCNC declared as its cardinal aim the desire "to achieve internal self-government for Nigeria whereby the people of Nigeria and the Cameroons under British Mandate shall exercise executive, legislative and judicial powers"- see, M. Crowder: *The Story of Nigeria* (London: Faber & Faber 1962).P.272.

13. See, Zik: *Selected Speeches of Dr. Nnamdi Azikiwe*(Oxford: Oxford University Press, 1961) p. 100.

14. For details of the composition of the conference, see Kalu Ezera; *Constitutional Developments in Nigeria*(London; Ind. Ed., 1964) pp. 107-109.

15. S.O. Osoba: "The Colonial Antecedents and Contemporary Development of Nigeria's Foreign Policy: A Study in the History of Social, Economic and Political Conflict," Moscow: Moscow State University, Unpublished Ph.D. Thesis, 1967, pp. 389-393.

16. Kalu Ezera: Constitutional Developments... p. 128.

17. For details of the formation of political parties in the North and the West, see the following: B.J. Dudley: *Parties and Politics in Northern Nigeria*(London: Frank Cass & Co. Ltd. 1968); P. C. Lloyd: "The Development of Political Parties in Western Nigeria," in *American Political Science Review* XLIX (3) 1955, pp. 693-707; J.S. Coleman: *Background to Nigerian Nationalism*(Berkely: University of California Press, 1958) pp. 343-352; 357-366.

18. G.O. Olusanya: "The Nationalist Movement in Nigeria", in O. Ikime (ed.): *Groundwork of Nigerian History*(London: Heinemann, 1980) pp. 566-567.

19. M. Crowder: *The Story of Nigeria*, p. 231

20. S.O. Osoba: "The Colonial Antecedents..." pp. 411-412.

21. Cited in, Ibid. p. 414.

22. *House of Representatives Debates* (Hereafter HRD) 31st March, 1953 p. 985.

23. Ibid., pp. 991-993.

24. See, O. Aluko "Politics of Decolonisation in British West Africa, 1945-1960," in Ajayi, J.F.A., and Crowder, M. (eds,): *History of West Africa*, vol.2 (London: Longman, 1974) p. 635.

25. *Ibid.*

26. *Ibid.*, p. 636

27. M. Okoye: *A Letter to Dr. Nnamdi Azikiwe* (Enugu: Fourth Dimension Publishers, 1979) p. 19.

28. See, Basil Davidson: *The Blackman's Burden: Africa and the Curse of the Nation- State*(Ibadan: Spectrum Books Ltd., 1993) p. 181.

29. F. A. O. Schwarz: *Nigeria: The Tribes, the Nation or the Race* (Cambridge: Massachusetts Institute of Technology Press 1965), p. 14.

30. Davidson: pp. 243-265.

31. See, B. E. Ate: "Influence Dynamics in Nigeria-United States Aid Relationship, 1960-1966," in *Nigeria Journal of International Studies*, 4(1&2), January and June 1980, p. 41.

32. Ibid.

33. O. Ojedokun: "The Future of Nigeria's Commonwealth Relations," in *Nigeria: Bulletin on Foreign Affairs* 1(4), May 1972, p. 14

34. Douglas Anglin: "Nigeria: Political Non-Alignment and Economic Alignment", in *Journal of Modern African Studies,* 2, July 1964, p. 247.

35. *Ibid.*

36. Terisa Turner: "Commercial Capitalism and the 1975 Coup", in Keith Panter –Brick(ed) *Soldiers and Oil: The Political Transformation of Nigeria*(London: Frank Cass, 1978) p. 167.

37. *Ibid.*

38 *Ibid,* pp. 168-172.

39. *Ibid.* p. 167

40. *Ibid.*

41. *Ibid.*

42. See *House of Representatives' Debates (HRD),* 18th November 1961, Cols. 3027-3030 and 3032; HRD, 2oth November, 1961, Cols. 3058-3060: *HRD* 29th

43. For more details, see B. J. Dudley:*Instability and Political Order: Politics and Crisis in Nigeria*(Ibadan: Ibadan University Press, 1973) pp. 1-86.

44. See, L. K. Jakande: *The Trial of Obafemi Awolowo*(London: Secker and Warbury, 1966).

45. See, *Africa Report,* March 1965, pp. 25-31.

46. There was organised destruction of lives and properties on a large scale under the infamous "operation wetie"-local slang for arson.

47. Robin Luckham: *The Nigerian Military: A Sociological Analysis of Authority and Revolt, 1960-1967.*(Cambridge: Cambridge University, 1971) p. 17.

48. See O. Achike: *Groundwork of Military Law and Military Rule in Nigeria* (Enugu: Forth Dimension Publishers, 1978).

49. See, N. J. Miners: *The Nigerian Army, 1956- 1966* (London: Methuen, 1971).

50. *Ibid.,* p. 2.

51. Said Adejumobi: "The Military as Economic Manager: The Babangida Regime and the Structural Adjustment Programme"-Unpublished Ph.D. Thesis, University of Ibadan, 1999, p. 68.

52. J. Bayo Adekanye: *Military Occupation and Social Stratification-An Inaugural Lecture*(Ibadan: Vantage Publisher (Int.) Ltd. 1993) pp. 6-8.

53. Adejumobi: The Military... p. 69.

54. Ibid.

55. Dudley: Instability... p. 171.

56. J. Bayo Adekanye: "Politics in a Military Context," in Peter P. Ekeh, Patrick Dele-Cole, and Gabriel O. Olusanya (eds); *Nigeria Since Independence: The First 25 Years* Vol. 1 (Politics and Constitutions) (Ibadan: Heinemann, for Nigeria since Independence History Project,1987) p. 190.

CHAPTER TWO

THE MILITARY'S INCURSION INTO NIGERIAN POLITICS: THE 'CORRECTIVE REGIME' CLAIM

INTRODUCTION

In the early hours of the 15ᵗʰ of January 1966 Nigeria's First Republic was terminated through a military putsch led by Major C. K. Nzeogwu. It was a bloody exercise in which the Prime Minister, Alhaji Abubakar Tafawa Balewa, the Premier of the Northern Region, Alhaji Ahmadu Bello, his counterpart in the Western Region, Chief Ladoke Akintola, the Minister for Finance, Chief Festus Okotie-Eboh and some high-ranking military officers were liquidated. The coup was successful in the North, partially successful in the West but failed in Lagos and the East. The Chief of Army Staff, Major General Aguiyi Ironsi, foiled the attempt in Lagos and eventually took over the reins of government from the largely stupefied civilian politicians[1]. This was the genesis of the first military administration in Nigeria. Previously, we have established that the First Republic was not only congenitally sick, but also that the political actors were parochial, unscrupulous, intolerant and inept[2]. We also held them partially responsible for politicising the military. They, therefore, created the context for military incursion into politics. This development shattered the myth of an apolitical military. However, another myth which presented the military as a corrective agency was adroitly substituted by the usurpers of power. Ever since the military started affecting a puritanic disposition especially at the inception of a new regime. The coup day broadcast speeches were always heavily-laden with condemnation of the activities of the deposed regime and prescriptions for sanitising the political terrain. In a well researched comparative study of

selected broadcast speeches of some civilian and military Heads
of Government in Nigeria, Eno Johnson established the frequent
use of the coercion/persuasion mix as two forms of compliance-
getting strategies[3]. She also affirmed that military leaders were
decidedly more coercive "especially so in their inaugural speeches"[4].
It is against this background that we shall examine the rhetorical
pronouncements and actions of the military regimes as a means
towards validating or invalidating (as the case may be) the corrective regime claim, and thereby establish their real intentions.

THE MILITARY AND POLITICS IN NIGERIA: A CORRECTIVE MISSION?

Major C. K. Nzeogwu declared, in his coup day broadcast to
the nation, that:

> Our enemies are the political profiteers, the swin-
> dlers, the men in high and low places that seek bribes
> and demand ten percent; those that seek to keep the
> country divided permanently so that they can remain
> in office as ministers, or VIPs at least, the tribalists,
> nepotists, those that make the country look big for
> nothing before international circles; those that have
> corrupted our society[5].

He went further to assert that the purpose of the coup was "to establish a strong, united and prosperous nation, free from corruption and
internal strife. (Our) method of achieving this is strictly military"[6].

Without doubt the dramatic termination of the life of the
corrupt and inept civilian administration and the coup day 'manifesto' of the planners enlivened hope in the future greatness of the
country. The euphoria that welcomed the coup announcement
attests to this[7]. Although it was not the planners and executors
of the coup that eventually formed the government, the image of
a corrective military regime had been etched in the minds of the
people. Perhaps if the coup planners had been allowed to form
the government or to put civilians of their choice there, may be
we would have witnessed better administration. Pointers to this
could be garnered from Major Nzeogwu's assertion that after

returning power to a set of responsible politicians "we would stand behind them with our fingers on the trigger"[8].

However, the point must be stressed that the military had been part and parcel of the governing class which it purports to correct and so cannot be totally abstracted from its ills. In particular, it must be remembered that the military had been a willing tool in the ruthless suppression of the Tiv revolts and it was even being prepared for the 'invasion' of the western region[9]- a development which the coup incident pre-empted. Arthur Nwankwo has argued that the 'Nzeogwu Movement' was revolutionary (at least at the level of intention) but that it was the failure of the coup "caused by Ironsi and Gowon's counter-offensive that re-constituted the *status quo*"[10]. However, since Nzeogwu and his group did not have the opportunity to rule it is difficult to affirm with reasonable exactitude that they would have revolutionised the polity.

Furthermore, the Ironsi regime that became the residuary legatee of the January putsch also laid claim to a revolutionary fervour by posing to be a corrective government. For instance in a communique issued by the Supreme Military Council (SMC), after its meeting of 7/8 June 1966, it was stated that, "(the) Military Government is not an elected government and must not be treated as such. It is a corrective government designed to remove the abuses of the old regime and to create a healthy community for a return to civilian government"[11]. As a practical demonstration of its commitment to reform, the Ironsi regime set in motion some reforming initiatives between June and July 1966. First, a Committee for National Reorientation was established under the chairmanship of Lt. Col. Anwuna. It was "to correct inefficiency, corruption and other laxities in the public services and national life"[12]. But the appointment of Lt. Col. Anwuna (an Igboman) as the Chairman "looked ominous to the Northerners"[13]. Second, tribunals of enquiry into Federal public corporations and the Lagos city council were established.

Third, it also legislated to investigate and confiscate ill-gotten assets under the old regime[14]. But these reforming initiatives were put up after the enactment of the unpopular Unification Decree

(Decree No. 34) of 23rd May 1966. Under this decree the regions were abolished and a unitary government was proclaimed for the nation. This was perceived as part of the corrective role of the military because of the belief that regionalism had promoted crisis and instability[15]. This move, however, further heightened suspicion of ethnic domination and so caused apprehension, especially in the North which had just lost the cream of her influential elite. It has been alleged in some quarters that the January coup was a clever design to foist Igbo hegemony over the country because the ring leaders of the coup were Igbo and General Ironsi who eventually became the head of the military regime was also Igbo. Not only were the coup planners not court martialled, Ironsi proceeded to surround himself with Igbo advisers and technocrats[16]. The deep-seated mistrust and the inability of the Ironsi regime "to take decisions which were either clear in their intentions or flexible in their application"[17], detracted from the credibility of the regime and its 'reforming initiatives'. Furthermore, the bloody manner in which the coup was executed had tacitly formalised violence as a means of transfer of power and sowed the seed of mutual suspicion and distrust within the military establishment. Four officers of Northern extraction had been killed in the coup whereas the East recorded no casuality. The West lost two officers and the Mid-West, one. The table below shows details of the number of officers killed and those that survived.

TABLE I: Number of Senior Officers* Killed and Surviving Coup of January 1966.

Region of Origin	Killed	Survived		Total
		Absent from Nigeria	In Nigeria	
North	4	0	1	5
West	2	2	2	6
Mid-West	1	1	1	3
East	0	0	7	7

* Rank of substantive Lt. Colonel and above, 1 January 1966.

Source: Robin Luckham, *The Nigerian Military: A Sociological Analysis of Authority and Revolt, 1960-67*. (London: Cambridge University Press, 1971), p. 43.

Thus, just as the situation was with the civilian casualities, the North also lost more officers than other regions. Understandably the Northern elements were ill at ease under the new dispensation and so were anxious to even scores and restore the political balance in their favour. Those of them in the army (mainly junior officers and NCOs) were apparently goaded into carrying out a reprisal action on 29th July, 1966. This counter coup reinforced the fact that the military had become seriously politicised and it also put paid to Ironsi's 'reforming initiatives'.

However, the way and manner in which the counter coup was executed further exacerbated the already volatile situation. The brutal assassination of Gen. Ironsi and Lt. Col. Adekunle Fajuyi, the Governor of the Western Group of provinces, and some prominent Igbo officers[18] created serious credibility problems for the emergent Lt. Col. Yakubu Gowon regime. The massacre of Igbo elements in the North and the apparent helplessness (or unwillingness) of the Federal Military Government (FMG) to halt the ethnic conflagrations casts doubts on its 'corrective regime' potentials at the outset. Matters came to a head on 30 May 1967 when the predominantly Igbo Eastern Region under the leadership of Lt. Col. Odumegwu Ojukwu opted to break away from the federation. A few days before this declaration, 27 May precisely, Gowon had broken the hitherto existing four regions into twelve states. This was a master stroke which served three major purposes for the Gowon regime.

First, through the state creation exercise, the yearnings of some minority elements in the regions had been partially satisfied. We can recall that some minority elements had been agitating for states of their own long before independence. The Calabar Ogoja Rivers (COR) movement and the United Middle Belt Congress (UMBC) had been at the forefront of such agitations intended to liberate the minority elements dominated by the three majority ethnic groups- the Hausa/Fulani in the North, the Yoruba in the West and the Igbo in the East. Thus, to the affected minority elements, Gowon's move was a kind of corrective measure, and this enlisted their support.

Second, the repudiation of unitary government and the restoration of federation through the state creation exercise showed a correct perception of the mood of the nation and this also allayed the prevalent fears of domination and marginalisation.

Third, as a result of the state creation exercise the former Eastern Region was split into three states (East Central, South East and Rivers States). This was a political masterstroke which ensured the confinement of the Igbo elements to the hinterland and freed the minority elements of any obligation to the rebel Republic of Biafra.

Without doubt the state creation exercise which could conceivably represent a corrective measure, secured for the Gowon regime some measure of legitimacy and popular acceptance. But, significantly the drift towards war could not be halted because of the uncompromising position of the adversaries[19]. The story of the Nigerian Civil War is too well known to warrant restating here. What is really of concern to us is how the civil war experience affected the military's corrective regime posturing. This came about in three major ways: first, the war was touted as a 'war of unity' and the populace was enjoined to contribute towards keeping Nigeria one. The successful prosecution of the war made the FMG more popular and stronger.

Second, the altruistic manner in which post-war rehabilitation and settlements were conducted forcefully brought the corrective image to the fore again. It will be recalled that at the conclusion of the war Gen. Gowon declared that there was "no victor, no vanquished"[20] since it was a war between brothers. Thus, the witch-hunting, recrimination and stigmatisation that usually come about after wars of this nature were noticeably absent in this case. This endeared the Gowon regime to the people such that,

> (For) a few years after the conclusion of the war, Gowon was still basking in the glory of its successful completion, so much that endearing slogans like, 'in unity we stand' and 'Go On With One Nigeria' (coined from his name) were rife across the country[21].

This led to "increased political and power consciousness on the part of the military"[22] generally while it also enabled the Gowon regime to extend its stay in the corridors of power for five more years after the war (making a total of nine years in government). This made the regime the longest serving military dispensation in Nigeria to date.

Third, as a result of its war experience and the antecedents, the issue of national security took on added significance thereby giving the military the excuse to exercise its coercive potentials to the fullest. For instance, the initially genial and humane Gowon turned, after the civil war, to a tyrant and a sit-tight dictator. Even when his regime was mis-managing the country's economy and becoming seriously enmeshed in corrupt practices, he 'dug in' and started to look for scapegoats within the civil society. Although this prolonged the life of the regime for a time, it dented the corrective image which the military had laboured to cultivate.

Apparently it was the desire to salvage that image that led to the General Muritala Mohammed coup of July 29, 1975 which swept Gen. Gowon from office. Mohammed's maiden speech alluded to this. He said, *inter alia:*

> After the civil war the affairs of state hitherto a collective responsibility, became characterized by lack of consultation, indiscipline and even neglect. Indeed the public at large became disillusioned and disappointed by these developments. *The trend was clearly incompatible with the philosophy and image of our corrective regime* (our emphasis)[23].

Mohammed followed up this declaration with some practical steps intended to restore that image. First, the seemingly untouchable Governors of the Gowon era were removed and their activities were subjected to probe. Ten of the twelve Governors were discovered to have misappropriated ten million Naira which they were ordered to refund[24]. Their known ill-gotten immovable assets were also confiscated.

The newly appointed Governors were made to understand that they were on military assignments and that they could be re-

assigned or removed if they failed to measure up to the standard expected of them[25]. They were no longer permitted to bring the affairs of their states to the Supreme Military Council (SMC), as the case was under Gowon. Such matters were now reserved for a subordinate body known as the Council of States. They were closely monitored by the office of the Chief of General Staff to which they were responsible. These measures strengthened the centre and also compelled the Governors to approach their assignments with a high sense of responsibility.

The style of leadership of Gen. Mohammed portrayed him as a humble friend of the masses. His openness, easy accessibility and less cumbersome security precautions were unprecedented. The governance system was also based on the collegiate style of administration which served as a kind of checks and balances against dictatorial tendencies[26]. This made it relatively easy for the regime to dispose of some lingering controversial issues without appearing to be partisan. One of such issues was the controversial census exercise of 1973 which Gowon used as an excuse for scuttling the transition programme, thereby prolonging the military's hold on political power. Gen. Mohammed promptly announced the cancellation of the 1973 census and a return to the 1963 census figures from which projections would be made for administrative and developmental purposes. This was a courageous decision given the fact that Mohammed hailed from the North which the 1973 census favoured most. However, the regime cleverly avoided getting involved in another census exercise by not putting it in its agenda.

The creation of additional states and the resiting of the federal capital were other serious issues that were speedily addressed by the Mohammed regime. It will be recalled that the creation of twelve states under Gowon was unilaterally done without consultation with the people. Thus, there were problems of unequal size and haphazard boundaries which the regime promised to refine later but procrastinated until Mohammed took over[27]. The new regime quickly established a five-man advisory committee to consult widely across the country and make recommendations

to the SMC on the matter. It was on this basis that the SMC took the decision to increase the number of states to nineteen with effect from the 6th of February 1976. This new arrangement ensured that the states were fairly equal in size.

A committee was also set up for the resiting of the federal capital. After an extensive tour, both at home and abroad, the committee recommended a centralised virgin site near Abuja to accommodate the proposed capital. This recommendation was accepted by the SMC and it promptly set in motion the necessary machineries for its actualisation[28].

It was, however, the regime's direct assault on corruption and indiscipline that showed its commitment towards correcting the prevalent ills of the society. There was a major shake up in which corrupt and redundant public servants and armed forces personnel were purged enmasse from the service[29]. But the exercise was superficial in that the roots of corruption were not reached. The overbearing influence of the neo-colonial state on the nation's economy was not seriously addressed and so the attraction of public office for personal gains did not diminish. The resort to drastic measures produced flashy but ephemeral results.

Furthermore, there were several allegations of victimisation during the 'house cleaning' exercise. For instance, the Chief Justice of the Federation, Dr. T. O. Elias, who was said to have been retired on health grounds[30] went forth to serve in the International Court of Justice at Hague for many years thereafter. There were also serious complaints about the social implications of the exercise[31]. The government responded by setting up the Col. Pedro Martins panel to look into the exercise. But the recommendations of the panel were not accepted by the government[32]. Whatever the case may be we must recognise the efforts of Mohammed as trail blazing to a very large extent. According to M. J. Dent,

> The Nigerian military failed to achieve any substantial measure of success in their goal of corrective government until the emergence of the regime headed by Muritala Mohammed after the overthrow of Gowon.

> The enormous respect, verging on adulation, for the
> memory of Mohammed thought (sic) Nigeria is a sure
> sign that, at least for the six months of his rule, Nigeria
> was set on the path of corrective government[33].

The subsequent transfer of power to civilians in October 1979 by Mohammed's successor (Gen. O. Obasanjo)[34], as earlier promised, also boosted the integrity of the military; the controversial nature[35] of the handover notwithstanding. But the civilian regime was in office for barely four years before it was sacked by another set of military leaders on the 31st of December 1983. The new regime headed by General Muhammadu Buhari was very rigid, coercive and repressive, all in an attempt to re-enact the corrective regime image. The regime never committed itself to a transfer of power to civilians instead it made moves to impose regimental orientations on the society. It was so obsessed with the idea of correcting the ills of the society that it enacted several draconian decrees (which shall be discussed elaborately in chapter four), instituted a War Against Indiscipline (WAI) and set aside the last Saturday of every month for environmental sanitation exercise nationwide.

This is not altogether strange because at the inception of new regimes the pressing desire to acquire legitimacy makes the military rulers to be very strict about efficiency, discipline and punctuality. It was a recurring experience to see latecomers in government offices locked out and humiliated or even sacked. According to Gutteridge "such actions helped to reinforce the popular impression of the military as patriotically dedicated to the public interest, as upright, honest and concerned about waste of time and money"[36]. Whereas, as Dent has rightly pointed out "the achievement of more total honesty (and dedication to duty-ours) requires the growth of a new ethic, or a change in the whole style of society"[37]. Any attempt to forcefully impose such attitudes on the people would only result in alienation and more devious negative attitudes as the case was during the Buhari era.

The Buhari regime unleashed a reign of terror on the people and this made it to lose face rapidly. To compound its problems

there were certain developments under it that were antithetical to its corrective regime posturing. First, three drug couriers (one of whom was retroactively convicted) were executed against the current of responsible public opinion and entreaties from well meaning Nigerians. This development sent a shock wave of alarm across the country. One would have thought that light imprisonment terms would have served the necessary purpose. Moreso, considering the facts that Nigeria was not the country of origin of the drugs and that drug addiction had not reached noticeable level in Nigeria. Even in places like the U. S. and some South American countries where the drug problem has reached alarming proportions, capital punishment has not been put in place. Little wonder then that instead of putting a stop to the 'drug problem' the execution achieved the opposite thereby popularising drug business on a wider scale[38].

Second, there was also the case of the fifty-three unopened suitcases, belonging to a highly placed Emir, stealthily brought into the country (with the connivance of government agents) during the week when the national currency was being changed. While addressing the press on this matter, the Finance Minister then, Dr. Onaolapo Soneye, admitted that "mistakes have been made and expected procedures by-passed"[39]. However, the same regime made sure that the maverick musician, Fela Anikulapo-Kuti, was jailed for bringing the proceeds of his overseas musical tour into the country in foreign currency. His action was deemed to have contravened the currency trafficking control decree. The point that we want to underscore here is that the regime was very selective and discriminatory in the application of its supposedly corrective measures.

Third, the Nigerian Security Organisation (NSO) was turned into an instrument of terror and intimidation reminiscent of the 'Gestapo' of the Hitler days. The organisation was employed to harass politicians (many of whom were harried into exile) and to intimidate the Press, Trade Unions and professional bodies, all in an attempt to correct the ills of the society. Also the two most prominent members of the regime (Buhari, the head

of state and Idiagbon, his second in command) were arrogant, unapproachable, constantly putting on very intimidating mien. All these were recipes for a coup which was masterminded by Gen. Ibrahim Babangida, the Chief of Army Staff.

In his maiden speech on the 27th of August 1985, Babangida rationalised the palace coup on the grounds that,

> (The) principles of discussion, consultation and cooperation which should have guided the decision making process of the Supreme Military Council and the Federal Executive Council were disregarded soon after the government settled down in 1984... it turned out that Major General Muhammadu Buhari was too rigid and uncompromising in his attitudes to issues of national significance... Major General Tunde Idiagbon was similarly inclined in that respect. He arrogated to himself absolute knowledge of problems and solutions, and acted in accordance with what was convenient to him, using the machinery of government as his tool[40].

The above statements implicitly suggest that the Babangida regime was equally out to correct some perceived wrongs and thereby revamp the image of the military.

To this end, Babangida made several populist pronouncements, repealed some unpopular decrees, released some jailed politicians and journalists, pledged to respect human rights and to effect a transfer of power to civilians[41.] The detention camps and the atrocious activities of the NSO were exposed for public condemnation. This was to prepare the ground for the reorganisation of the body. There was also a promise to reform the police and put a stop to corrupt activities across board. These earned for the Babangida regime the much needed legitimacy and popular acceptance.

However, after settling down in office he reneged on his promises. He carried out more dastardly acts than his predecessors, albeit in a more suave manner. Under Babangida, ethno-religious crises reached alarming proportions and nearly tore the country apart on several occasions. This was partly a consequence

of some of the religious policies of that administration which fostered a divide and rule system of governance. For instance, his regime clandestinely enrolled Nigeria as a member of the Organisation of Islamic Conference (OIC) in 1986. This was in flagrant disregard for Nigeria's secular status. But it was obviously intended to enlist the support of some powerful ethno-religious configurations. More importantly, he bastardised the economy through impious experimentations, like the introduction of the infamous Structural Adjustment Programme (SAP), which left the majority of the people pauperised and the rich few richer still. He therefore created conditions that could encourage the launching of coups. And, in fact, there were two publicised failed attempts under him. These were the Vasta coup of December 1985 and the Orkar coup of April 1990. The perpetrators of both coup attempts were summarily dealt with in order to serve as a deterrent to others nursing similar ambitions. Thus, he was able to remain in office for eight years (1985 – 1993) thereby making his regime the second longest serving military regime in Nigeria.

THE SIGNIFICANCE OF THE CORRECTIVE REGIME POSTURING

One overriding fact that has emerged from the discussion so far is that for as long as Nigeria's economy remained prostrate and its politics unstable there was always something to correct and this provided excuse for military men to seize power. The recurring incident of coups and counter coups, however, exposed the lie in the corrective regime posturing of the military rulers. There are two sides to this observation. First, it has shown that the military organisation had become a nurturing ground for individuals and cliques who readily appropriated its machinery for satisfying selfish political ambitions. Second, similar allegations to the ones usually levelled against deposed civilians were also levelled against their fallen compatriots. In fact, with the possible exemption of the Murtala Mohammed regime, successive regimes always left the nation worse than they met it.

Perhaps it should be emphasised too that corrective measures or sanctions can only be meaningful and effective if those initiating and administering them are known to be above board. According to Lt. Gen. Danjuma, the military in Nigeria is known to be "corrupt, permeated by secret societies and protection rackets"[42]. The civil war period up to the time of the advent of Mohammed was replete with several corrupt practices, especially in arms procurement, pay rackets and outright embezzlement of government funds[43]. And even after the sanitising exercise of 1975 (especially with the demise of Gen. Mohammed) the situation soon returned to the former ways. By the time of the Babangida regime, corruption had become all-pervading and almost institutionalised. He tacitly endorsed the practice of 'settlement'[44] in 'oiling' official transactions and operated generally with the conviction that anybody could be bought over if the price was right[45].

From the foregoing, it is obvious that the military did not justify its claim to puritanism. Even the cleansing exercise under Gen. Mohammed was too superficial to make any lasting impact on the body politic. Whatever gains that were made at this period were rubbished under the Babangida dispensation. In sum, it must be emphasised that the military in Nigeria is not endowed with any special quality that could make it to step at will into any legitimacy vacuum created through the ineptitude of its civilian counterparts. It only capitalised on its monopoly of the instruments of coercion and its arrogation of superior vision to forcefully push itself into political reckoning. Thereafter it projected a puritanic disposition in order to live up to the image of a corrective regime.

The strategy served some useful purposes for the military regimes. First, it was useful in rationalising and legitimising the military's intrusion into politics. Second, it gave support to the arrogation of superior vision vis-à-vis the civilian counterparts. And, third, it provided the context for the clamp-down on anti-military and pro-democracy elements in the polity. But this strategy was not enough to guarantee military political domi-

nance for that long. There were other complementary strategies, more of secondary nature, that co-jointly sustained the military in power. One of such strategies was the neo-patrimonial system of governance which most of the regimes adopted. It is to this that we now turn our attention in the next chapter.

Notes

1. See, Robin Luckham: *The Nigerian Military: A Sociological Analysis of Authority and Revolt, 1960-67* (London: Cambridge University Press 1971) pp. 17-51.
2. See Chapter One above.
3. R. Eno Johnson: "A Comparative Study of Selected Broadcast Speeches of Civilian and Military Heads of Government in Nigeria"-Unpublished Ph. D Thesis, University of Ibadan, 1988. pp. 247-248.
4. Ibid. p. 256.
5. See A. Ademoyega: *Why We Struck: The Story of the First Nigerian Coup* (Ibadan: Evans Brothers, 1981) p. 89.
6. Ibid.
7. See, the National Dailies of 16th and 17th January 1966.
8. Quoted in, Luckham:... p. 285.
9. See, R. Anifowoshe: *Violence and Politics in Nigeria: The Tiv and Yoruba Experience* (New York/Enugu: Nok Publishers, 1982).
10. Arthur Nwankwo: *The Military Option to Democracy: Class, Power and Violence in Nigerian Politics* (Enugu: Fourth Dimension Pub. Ltd, 1987) p. 166.
11. Quoted in, Luckham: ... p. 281.
12. Ibid. p. 277.
13. Ibid.
14. Ibid.
15. See, W. F. Gutteridge: *Military Regimes in Africa,* (London: Methuen Co. Ltd., 1975) p.102.
16. See, T. Mohammed and M. Haruna: "The Civil War", in Oyeleye Oyediran (ed.): *Nigerian Government and Politics Under Military Rule, 1966-79,* (Lagos: Friends Foundation. Publishers Ltd., 1988). p. 27.

37. Dent, p. 13

38. See, *African Concord,* March 25, 1991

39. See, *African Guardian,* January 8, 1990. p. 14.

40. See, *Newswatch* Sept. 9, 1985, p. 18, and, *West Africa,* Sept. 2, 1985, p. 1791.

41. See, O. Olagunju and S. Oyovbaire: *Portrait of a New Nigeria; Selected Speeches of IBB, Vol. 1,* (Lagos: Precision Press, n.d.) pp. 21-26.

42. Quoted in, Dent: p. 114

43. For details of the corrupt practices within the military, See, Oluleye: Military Leadership... pp. 156-166.

44. An oblique reference to 'Bribery'

45. This was in the manner of Machiavelli's conjectural 'Prince'.

17. Luckham:... pp. 277-278.

18. For details of the death toll, see, James Ojiako: *13 Years of Military Rule* (Lagos: Daily Times of Nigeria, 1979) pp. 38 & 40.

19. See, G. Ugochukwu. Nwokeji: "Ojukwu's Leadership and the Nigerian Civil War", in *Ife Journal of History,* 2(1), 1995, pp. 72-89.

20. See, NAI/SN/42 – *Civil War Bulletin: No Victors, No Vanquished.*

21. Toyin Falola, A. Ajayi, A. Alao and B. Babawale: *The Military Factor in Nigeria, 1966 – 1985* (Lewiston/Queenston/Lampeter: The Edwin Mellen Press, 1994) p. 7.

22. Said Adejumobi: "The Impact of the Civil War on the State" in Siyan Oyeweso (ed.): *Perspectives on the Nigerian Civil War,* (Lagos: OAP Humanities Press, 1992) p. 231.

23. See, James Ojiako: 13 Years... p. 29.

24. See, M. J. Dent: "Corrective Government: Military Rule in Perspective", in Keith Panter-Brick(ed.): *Soldiers and Oil: The Political Transformation of Nigeria,* (London:: Frank Cass, 1978) p. 114.

25. The Governor of Western State Navy Capt. Akin Aduwo, was replaced within two weeks of his appointment because of "insufficient determination". See, Ibid.

26. Ibid. p. 116

27. Ibid., p. 125.

28. Ibid.

29. For details, See, Ojiako:... pp. 89-129.

30. Ibid, p. 91

31. See, James Oluleye: *Military Leadership in Nigeria, 1966-1979* (Ibadan: University Press Ltd., 1985) pp. 243-244.

32. See, NAI/CE/M13A- *MARTINS, Col. Msgr. P,* Federal Military Government's Views on the Report and Recommendations of the Panel on the Social Implications of the 1975 Retirement Exercise, by Col. Msgr. P. Martins and others.

33. Dent: p. 102.

34. On the 13th of February 1976 Gen. Mohammed was assassinated in a bloody abortive coup attempt. His second in command, Gen. Obasanjo, replaced him as the Head of State and Commander-in-Chief of the Armed Forces.

35. See, Chapter Five below.

36. Gutteridge: *Military Regimes...* p. 123

CHAPTER THREE

THE POLITICS OF PATRONAGE AND SUBORDINATION

INTRODUCTION

We have noted previously from Sandbrook that patrimonialism has always been a feature of African politics[1]. But until the advent of the military into politics it was confined to ethnic and primordial associational ties. Under the military it assumed a wider dimension which transcended ethnic ties but still based on patron-client relationships. This manifested in the form of contracts, appointments, promotions and other forms of rewards for loyal supporters either in the military or in the civil society, irrespective of ethnic background. Under this neo-patrimonial arrangement the 'military in government' was the patron while the clients were the beneficiaries of government patronage.

Military rulers in Nigeria perfected with time a network of patron-client relations spanning social, economic and political terrains. The concentration of national resources at the center where the military's grip was most profound enabled it to ascribe a paternalistic role to itself in Nigeria's political power play. It also assisted it in 'pocketing' its civilian counterparts through the opening up of several avenues for private accumulation. This fostered collusion between the military oligarchies and the civilian surrogates in foisting military regimes on the nation. The process was assisted by the incidence of the civil war and the attendant policies and actions at the federal level which enhanced the influence of the military and the centrality of the state in Nigeria's politics.

A complementary development in the post war period was the incidence of the 'oil boom', in the mid-1970s, which enriched

state coffers beyond imagination. Since all the revenues that accrued to the nation first went to the federal government at the center, it thus had exclusive access to a burgeoning resources pool which it distributed anyway it deemed fit. Richard Joseph has rightly observed that, "the state assumed the capacity to determine not only *Who* gets *What*, *When* and *How*, but the very nature of the *What* around which the scramble would ensue"[2]. Thus, "when the state itself becomes the key distributor of financial resources – and this in the absence of any socialist ideology – all government projects ... become submerged by the intense pressures for the conversion of those projects into means of individual and group appropriation"[3].

Before the advent of the military the federating regions in Nigeria were largely self sustaining in terms of control over revenue generation and appropriation for their developmental needs. Thus, the influence of the federal government was minimally felt. But beginning with the Yakubu Gowon regime, the situation was drastically reversed in favour of the federal government. Successive military regimes since then de-emphasised the principle of derivation in respect of both oil and non-oil revenues. A new arrangement by which the federal government transferred revenue to the states through the Distributable Pool Account (DPA) was entrenched. For instance, portions of customs and excise duties hitherto paid to the States on the basis of derivation were transferred to the DPA as from 1st April, 1975[4]. In addition the royalties accruing to state governments on the same basis (i.e. derivation) were reduced from 45 to 20 percent[5].

Furthermore revenue allocation formula under different regimes were skewed in favour of the federal government. The trend is graphically captured in the table below.

TABLE II: Recommendation On Shares Of Federal Revenues by Level Of Government (%): Commissions /Committees /Reports /Acts

LEVEL OF GOVERNMENT	Aboyade (1978)	Okigbo (1980)	Allocation of Revenue (Federation Account, etc). Act, 1981
Federal	57	53	55
States	30	30	35
Local	10	10	10
Special Fund	3	7	*

*   Special Fund consisting 1.5% for the development of mineral producing areas and 1% of ecology is included in the 35% State Allocation.

Source: Bade Onimode, "Resources Derivation, Allocation and Utilization", in *Constitutions and Federalism-Conference Proceedings* (Lagos: Friedrich Ebert Foundation, 1997) P. 185.

Although the information provided in this table is only up to 1981, it is important to note that from then (i.e. 1981) to 1993 the situation remained virtually the same. We recognize the fact that in 1989 the Babangida regime increased the share of local governments to 15% which was further increased to 20% in 1992[6]. It is instructive to note that the additional revenue given to the local governments were subtracted mostly from the share of the states while the federal government continued to retain the greatest share. This policy orientation ensured that the military regimes had enough prebends for appropriation and distribution to support groups and pliable opponents.

And, for those who could not be pocketed through neo-patrimonial contrivances a supplementary strategy of subordination through certain strong-arm measures was employed in a kind of 'carrot and stick' style of governance. The manipulation of postings, promotions, retirements, dismissals and other punitive measures in order to elicit support and compliance constitute the politics of subordination. The two (i.e. patronage and subordination) were regularly employed by the military regimes but

in varying degrees, depending on the prevailing circumstances. Under the Babangida dispensation the twin-strategy was maximally utilized to shore-up that regime in power for eight years.

In this chapter an attempt will be made to examine the forms and dynamics of the neo-patrimonial or patronage system alongside with the indices of the politics of subordination. This will be undertaken in two parts corresponding with the major divisions in the society. These are the 'military' and the 'civil society'.

PATRONAGE AND SUBORDINATION: THE MILITARY CONSTITUENCY AT THE RECEIVING END

A major problem that a new military regime usually contends with is that of how to manage the latent antagonism between the "military in government" and the "military in the barracks". The conflicting interests of both parties have often become "the basic cause of many counter coup attempts, conspiracies, and threats to which such regimes are so vulnerable"[7]. Although this problem could diminish with the commencement of mutually agreed upon disengagement/transition programmes, it does not disappear completely. For, as Adekanye has rightly observed, intra-officer conflicts deriving from "unequal service conditions in the area of pay, privilege, promotion and other self-regarding interests are (also) known to spill over into acts and/or threats of coups and countercoups against government"[8]. For instance, the abortive coup of 13 February 1976 in which the head of state, General Mohammed, was assassinated has been linked to misgivings over some of these factors[9]. In addition, the military government could also be confronted with intra-officer conflicts over demilitarization and democratization. There was, therefore, the need to evolve tactics and strategies for containing the "military in the barracks" and for reinforcing the "military in government".

Generally, in order to stave-off coups and ensure concerted efforts in foisting military oligarchies over the nation, nearly all military regimes in Nigeria made attempts to pamper 'loyal' members of their primary constituency through accelerated promotions, political appointments and special welfare packages.

The familiar pattern was that, whenever a military regime seized power, the conspirators and their supporters usually proceeded to share strategic and political posts. A super-ordinate Military Council, known at different times as Supreme Military Council (SMC); Armed Forces Ruling Council (AFRC); National Defence and Security Council (NDSC); and Provisional Ruling Council (PRC) made up of a few high ranking loyal officers, was usually constituted as the highest ruling body (at least in theory).

Military Governors were also appointed for the States and other 'deserving' officers were appointed as Federal Commissioners or Ministers, Board Chairmen and controllers of various Task Force committees. Gen. Babangida put the matter succinctly when he asserted that, "(For) every group or class of officers who got involved in changing a government, as much as possible you carry them along. And when you do, you have the duty to promote them, to give them assignments so that unity would remain"[10]. This has been the orientation since the inception of military rule in Nigeria. Even under the 'exceptional' Mohammed dispensation, within five months of taking over power (precisely on 8 January 1976), and shortly after the mass purge of the services, sixteen senior officers of the regime, including the head of state, were made Generals. Reproduced below is the list of the beneficiaries and the effective date of the promotion[11].

NO	BENEFICIARIES	NEW RANKS	EFFECTIVE DATE
1	Brigadier Muritala Mohammed	General	w.e.f*. 29/7/75
2	Brigadier Olusegun Obasanjo	Lt. General	w.e.f. 29/7/75
3	Brigadier T.Y. Danjuma	Lt. General	w.e.f. 1/1/76
4	Commodore M.A. Adelanwa	Rear-Admiral	w.e.f. 1/1/76
5	Colonel J. Yisa-Doko	Air Commodore	w.e.f. 1/1/76
6	Brigadier E.O. Abisoye	Major General	w.e.f 1/1/76
7	Brigadier M. Adamu	Major general	w.e.f 1/1/76
8	Brigadier J.A. Akinrinmade	Major General	w.e.f. 1/1/76
9	Brigadier O.E. Obada	Major General	w.e.f. 1/1/76
10	Brigadier G.S. Jalo	Major General	w.e.f. 1/1/76
11	Brigadier O. Olutoye	Major General	w.e.f. 1/1/76
12	Brigadier I.D.Bisalla	Major General	w.e.f. 1/1/76

13	Brigadier M. Shuwa	Major General	w.e.f. 1/1/76
14	Brigadier I.B.M. Haruna	Major General	w.e.f. 1/1/76
15	Brigadier J.J. Oluleye	Major General	w.e.f. 1/1/76
16	Brigadier H.E.O. Adefope	Major General	w.e.f 1/1/76

- w.e.f. – with effect from.

In his defence of the new promotions, the Chief of Army Staff, Lt. Gen. Theophilus Danjuma, stated that Nigerian army officers were 'rank shy' in the past whereas the number of army officers was "below establishment"[12]. But it should be noted that the timing of the promotions and the set of people who benefitted from the exercise suggest political motives as well.

This trend continued under subsequent regimes up to the time of Gen. Babangida when promotions, postings, appointments and retirements in the military were maximally exploited to secure loyalty. Then it was not uncommon to hear of the retirement of recently promoted officers or even the promotion of recently retired officers. There were also instances of retired officers compensated with or made to retain political appointments. As a result of the inter-locking nature of these developments, they are taken together in the illustrative accounts that follow.

In October 1986 Babangida's first Chief of General Staff (CGS), Commodore Ebitu Ukiwe, was removed and replaced by the erstwhile Chief of Naval Staff, Augustus Aikhomu. Rear Admiral Patrick Koshoni was appointed the new Chief of Naval Staff. Alhaji Muhammadu Gambo became the new Inspector General of Police (IGP) on the mandatory retirement of Etim Inyang. The other Service Chiefs already appointed since 1985 were: Major General Sanni Abacha (who played a very prominent role in the coup that brought Babangida to power) as Chief of Army Staff; Air Vice Marshal Ibrahim Alfa as the Chief of Air Staff; and, Major General Domkat Bali as the Chairman of the Joint Chiefs of Staff as well as the Defence Minister. In this way the top notchers of the clique that brought Babangida to power were compensated.

Furthermore, on 1st October 1987 this set of influential officers were promoted as part of the activities marking the 27th Inde-

pendence Anniversary celebrations. President Babangida also promoted himself from Major General to full General (skipping the position of Lt. Gen.) while the CGS, Rear Admiral Aikhomu and the Defence Minister, who also doubled as the Chairman Joint Chiefs of Staff, Major General Domkat Bali, were elevated to the ranks of Vice Admiral and Lt. General respectively. The Service Chiefs, Major Gen. Sanni Abacha (Army), Rear Admiral Patrick Koshoni (Navy) and Air Vice Marshal Ibrahim Alfa became Lt. General, Vice Admiral and Air Marshal respectively[13]. Surprisingly by December 1989 three of the Service Chiefs – Koshoni (Navy), Alfa (Airforce) and Gambo (Police) had been retired. Their replacements were Vice Admiral Murtala Nyako; Air Marshal Nureini Yusuf and Aliyu Attah. Following the resignation of Lt. Gen. Bali from government and his voluntary retirement from service, Bali's other portfolio – defence minister- was taken over by Babangida himself[14].

The misgiving generated by these jugglings especially the treatment meted out to Lt. Gen. Bali in order to subordinate him and the 'Langtang Mafia' which he represented[15] caused uneasiness in government circles and threatened to discredit the government. Babangida had to quickly initiate 'fence-mending' moves one of which was the post-retirement promotion of Bali to General and the offer of ministerial appointment which he (Bali) declined[16]. Bali subsequently addressed a press conference which revealed a lot about Babangida's 'maradonic' traits. This incident was significant in two major respects. First, it caused division in the military – a situation which Babangida had always wanted to prevent. Second, it was also a pointer to the fact that in as much as Babangida was prepared to do away with or render ineffective anybody who had finished serving his purpose, he was still very careful not to widen the circle of 'enemies' unnecessarily. It is within this context that we can appreciate why some influential top military officers like Generals Ike Nwachukwu, Yohanna Kure, Gado Nasko, Mamman Kotangora still held ministerial appointments long after retirement from service.

The most striking example of Babangida's ingenuity in the manipulation of promotion, retirement and appointments for political gains was that of Aikhomu. When Babangida was under pressure to demonstrate his commitment to the transition programme by appointing a civilian Vice President, he promptly retired Aikhomu (the CGS) and appointed him as the Vice President. Aikhomu also bagged a post-retirement promotion to the rank of full Admiral in order to assuage his feelings and placate his admirers. In this way Babangida was literally "eating his cake and having it". Although it can be argued with justification that the spate of retirements[17] under Babangida was part of 'load shedding' considered necessary for "preparing the forces for the challenges of the 1990s and beyond"[18]. Babangida needed such moves to take care of the problems of political security and survival[19].

The issues of political security and survival had always been central to Babangida's political calculations from the very beginning. Early in his regime middle level officers (Majors and Lt. Cols.), who were generally known to be highly prone to planning and executing coups, were focused upon for appointments as Governors and Task Force Chairmen[20]. Some of the early beneficiaries were Majors Mohammed Umar and Lawan Gwadabbe, and Lt. Cols Yohanna Madaki and Tanko Ayuba who were known to harbour radical views. Later in the life of the regime, officers of the rank of Colonel and Brigadiers were made to take over as General Officer Commanders (GOCs), directors or commanders of the army medical corps, finance and accounts, training and operations, training and doctrine, staff duties and planning, school of infantry, supply and transport and educational corps[21]. These were officers who had proved their loyalty in their initial posts/appointments early in the life of the regime.

We can also recall the movement, in 1987, of the 242 Recce Batallion from Ibadan to the Brigade of Guards in Lagos under the watchful eyes of the Chief of Army Staff and the Commander-in-Chief of the Armed Forces. This was a highly expedient move considering the fact that the Recce Batallion was a highly rated and very mobile unit having the largest number of armoured vehicles

in the Nigerian army.[22] Such an important unit should be under close monitoring because of its potential for destabilization.

Still on the issue of security and survival Babangida was prepared at anytime to sacrifice any officer that fell foul of his political calculations. Apart from the summary execution of real and imaginary coup plotters, intended primarily to serve as deterrent to would-be plotters, some officers were dismissed from service for similar offences and also in order to appease some powerful political configurations. For instance, Col Yohanna Madaki, military governor of Gongola State, was dismissed from service because of his disdainful treatment of the Emir of Muri, who was alleged to be involved in some fraudulent practices[23]. The other reason for his dismissal was his romantic recall of late Nzeogwu's exploits in a press interview. This conjured painful memories in the North as Nzeogwu was responsible for the assassination of their reverred Premier, Alhaji Ahmadu Bello, in the January 1966 putsch. Although Madaki's dismissal was later converted to retirement with full benefits, the necessary political purpose had been served. Babangida was also reputed to be highly sociable in military circles and generous to the officers. Their lives were touched by Babangida's legendary generosity on important occasions like marriages, birthdays, new births and deaths, religious festivals, etc. Many of them also received cash and car gifts; sponsorship for medical treatment abroad and across-the-board increases in pay for military personnel generally[24]. Furthermore, some military officers enjoyed several privileges that were totally out of alignment with either their level of responsibility or the prevailing economic situation in the country. The most striking example was the so-called 'special welfare package' (outside the service scheme) under which cars worth more than N500 million were purchased for some armed forces personnel in 1991/92[25].

In addition the federal military government since the days of Gen. Gowon had been expending huge sums of money on welfare services like construction of modern barracks in the state capitals, establishment of special schools for children and wards of military personnel and subsidized medical facilities. All

these were possible because of the huge allocations to the defence sector under succeeding military regimes. For instance, defence which accounted for a mere 6 percent of government expenditure before the advent of military rule, averaged 33 percent between 1967 and 1970 (the war years) and fell to 12 percent in 1975, which "is still about double that of peace time era"[26].

Although the relative shares of federal expenditures on defence started declining after the war, in absolute terms defence spending actually continued to rise. By 1987 it claimed nearly 10 percent of federal expenditures when the budgetary allocation exceeded 2 Billion Naira. The situation remained virtually at this level for the remaining period of the Babangida regime. The situation is captured in the table below:

TABLE III: Defence Share of Total Federal Nigerian Expenditures Under Babangida

Fiscal year	Total federal Expenditures (Millions of Naira)	Total Defence Expenditures (Millions of Naira)	Percent of Total Federal Expenditure		
			Defence	Education	Health
1985	14,894.6	1.385.2	9.3	5.4	1.4
1986	16,733.3	803.2	4.8	5.2	1.9
1987	22,018.7	2,154.9	9.8	2.0	0.6
1988	27,749.5	1,720.1	6.2	6.4	2.0
1989	41,028.3	2,219.3	5.4	8.3	1.9
1990	60,268.2	2285.2	3.7	4.6	1.3
1991	66,584.4	2,711.7	4.0	2.3	1.1
1992	92,797.4	4821.8	5.2	2.6	1.7
1993	177,310.2	6,381.6	3.5	3.5	1.4

Sources:

(i)   CBN-*STATISTICAL BULLETIN*, vol. 3 No. 1, June 1992, Pp. 97 and 100.

(ii) CBN - *Annual Report and Statement of Accounts for the year ended 31st December 1993,*, Pp. 62 and 64.

(iii) CBN - *Annual Report and Statement of Accounts for the year ended 31st December 1994*, Pp. 56 and 57.

Furthermore, the high-handedness and corrupt activities of those occupying political offices were often connived at even when the incriminating evidences were overwhelming. For instance, under Gowon's regime, ten of the twelve military governors were seriously enmeshed in corrupt practices. Yet they were retained in office without censorship[27]. It took the intervention of the Mohammed regime to unseat them. But this only created room for another set of military governors. Under the Babangida dispensation, military governors were appointed and replaced many times not so much for corrupt practices as for the need to allow many loyal officers to benefit from the largesse associated with that exalted political office.

Retired military officers were also not forgotten in the drive to secure the loyalty and support of the military constituency. For instance, in July 1986 (barely one year into the Babangida administration) the office of the Chief of Army staff dispatched a circular requesting State Governors and some selected federal ministries to give special consideration to retired military officers in the award of contracts. The affected ministries were those of Internal Affairs; Communications; Information, Youth, Sports, and Culture; Transport and Aviation; Labour and Productivity; and Trade[28]. As part of the rehabilitation efforts, DIFRRI operations in the different states of the federation were put under the control and supervision of retired military officers.

An attempt was also made by the Babangida regime to bridge the communication gap between the military government and the military in the barracks through the establishment of the Armed Forces Consultative Assembly (AFCA) in 1989. The Assembly was made up of 146 members from the Nigerian Army (mainly battalion and brigade commanders and sergeant –majors); 40 members from the Navy (including the equivalent of three regimental sergeant-majors); 47 members from the Air Force (including officers and non-commissioned officers); 7 members from the joint headquarters of the armed forces; and, 25 members from the Police (including the force sergeant-major from the force headquarter)[29]. The members were to serve as the

link between the officers and the other ranks. Briefings were to be held at regular "Durbars" (a kind of peoples' parliament) in the barracks[30]. Although Gen. Babangida described the Assembly as a complementary forum for governance during the transition period[31], it was a convenient way to shield the rank and file from being infested with the prevalent agitation in the civil society. It was also a means of monitoring this class of military personnel and to ensure that they tow the line in the perennial 'war' against the progressively radicalised civil society. The establishment of the AFCA only shortly after the anti-SAP riots of May 1989, which nearly brought the administration to its knees, lend credence to these assertions. This leads us to the examination of the forms and dynamics of the politics of patronage and subordination as applied to the civil society.

THE PATRONAGE SYSTEM AND THE CIVIL SOCIETY

The politics of patronage and subordination was also employed in controlling and enlisting the support of the civil society. This manifested in many ways, one of which was the regular cooptation of influential civilians into government through appointments into sinecure (albeit, subordinate) posts. Respected jurists, academics, politicians, retired military officers, businessmen and journalists were successfully induced to take up appointments under different military regimes thereby conferring credibility on such regimes. The trend began under the Gowon regime when at its inception Gowon released some jailed politicians and proceeded to appoint some of them into important positions in his administration.

A striking example in this regard was that of Chief Obafemi Awolowo, the widely acclaimed leader of the Yoruba and the opposition leader in the government of the first republic, who had been jailed on trumped-up charges of treasonable felony in 1963. His release from prison and subsequent appointment as the federal commissioner (minister) for finance and the vice-chairman of the federal executive council was a masterstroke which tacitly enlisted the support of the Yoruba for the Gowon regime

in its early days. It should be noted that Gowon was not accepted by the Igbo of the Eastern region because of the circumstances that surrounded his coming to power[32]. Therefore the support of the Yoruba in the West was very crucial for his political security and survival. Some other influential politicians who were coopted into the administration included, Mr. Joseph Tarka (from Tiv in the Middle Belt), Alhaji Aminu Kano (a popular grassroot politician from the North); Alhaji Shehu Shagari (who was to later become the President of Nigeria in the second republic); just to mention a few. This practice continued under succeeding regimes to the extent that it soon became standard practice for civilians to be lobbying or even hustling for appointments at the inception of new regimes. This was usually done through the agency of notable traditional rulers and influential military officers.

As a result of the increasing number of people to be coopted, it soon became necessary for military rulers to create more posts in the form of the establishment of irrelevant parastatals, commissions, ad-hoc committees and boards often times duplicating the services of already established ministries. Some examples of such bodies included, National Sports Commission, Directorate of Mass Mobilisation for Social Justice and Economic Recovery (MAMSER), Directorate of Food, Roads and Rural Infrastructure (DIFRRI), Center for Democratic Studies (CDS), Better Life Programme (BLP), Peoples' Bank (PB) etc. These and many more proved to be conduit pipes for servicing private interests.

For instance, between 1990 and 1991, the CDS that was established to tutor politicians on democratic ethos, got the sum of N29,583,095.00 from the presidency[33]. Between 1986 and 1992, DIFRRI expended N1,925,848,083.68[34] on hardly perceptible rural development. MAMSER was said to have expended N390,421,654.00 on mobilisation between 1987 and 1991[35]. There are no enduring legacies for all these expenses. However, they reinforced the patron-client relationship and the paternalistic role of the military.

The military rulers also penetrated the press sucking in some of its members regularly through bribes (known as 'Brown Enve-

lope' in local parlance) and windfalls from government-spon-
sored paid advertisements and supplements. Journalists were also
regularly coopted into government as press secretaries, personal
assistants and hired writers. Soremekun's observations on mili-
tary-press relationship is worth highlighting here. He said,

> (At) the dawn of every military regime... the News-
> papers are usually full of enthusiastic editorials
> and reports praising the new regime to the high
> havens(sic) and ultimately as is usually the case, a few
> visible figures in the media get invited to serve as
> commissioners, ministers or advisers[36].

And,

> (In) relatively recent time the military establishment
> has evolved sophisticated procedures for sucking in
> journalists. Thesecome in the form of press briefings
> and a relatively privileged state house correspondent-
> corps, which is certainly not materially poorer for its
> proximity to power[37].

However, the relationship was not totally cordial. Some sections
of the Press (especially privately-owned print media) did not only
prove to be incorruptible but they were unrelenting in demystify-
ing the military. This did not go down well with military dictators
who proceeded to employ several strong-arm measures to deal
with the few recalcitrant elements[38]. But the fact remains that such
people were in the minority. A large segment of the Press (print
and electronic media) was bought over. For instance, on August30,
1975 the federal military government announced the acquisition
of 60% and 100% equities of the Daily Times of Nigeria Ltd. and
the New Nigeria Newspaper Ltd. respectively. This was carried out
through the agency of the government- owned National Insurance Corporation of Nigeria (NICON)[39]. Ever since these two
highly influential print media became 'mouth organs' of military
governments. And, of course, until 1992 all the electronic media
in Nigeria were owned by the government. We can recall that on
24th August 1992 the Babangida regime established the National
Broadcasting Commission (NBC) to screen the applications of

private organizations that intended to establish electronic media. This paved way for the licensing of private broadcasting houses in Nigeria [40]. But it had a lot of implications for information dissemination and propaganda.

In the case of trade unions, the approach was more subtle. The move to curtail their activities began in 1978 with the merger of several unions under one umbrella organization known as the Nigerian Labour Congress (NLC)[41]. There is no doubting the fact that this development was intended to make trade unions pro-government as the following statement by a senior staff of the Cabinet Office, Lagos (Mr. F.U. Kaueven) suggests:

> ... There is need for cooperation between government and trade unions to identify and root out subverts from the midst of the labour force... If it is Trade Union Executives who spot subverts within their Unions they should not hesitate to alert their government's security forces. If it is the security forces who identify these subverts,they will (sic) solicit the cooperation of Union executives to eliminate them from the mids (sic) of labour unions[42].

The first manifestation of the military government's keen interest in the affairs of labour unions was the 1978 merger exercise referred to earlier. This was followed by the evolution of some instruments of law designed to contain the unions. These were the Industrial Arbitration Panel (IAP) and National Industrial Court (NIC)[43]. These 'hurdles' were expected to be scaled before the unions could declare a strike action.

And when it appeared as if these measures would not yield satisfactory results, the military government started intervening directly in the affairs of the NLC, especially in the election to the executive posts. For instance, in 1988, it appointed Mr. Kayode Ogunkoya as the sole administrator of the NLC after a failed attempt to upstage the Ali Chiroma – led executive in an election during the Delegates' Conference in Benin[44]. The 'government's candidate', Comrade Shamang, could not muster enough votes to gain control. But he generated enough crisis that provided the

context for rationalizing the imposition of a sole administrator on the beleaguered body. The sole administrator's term of office was extended twice until when the auguries favoured the election of a 'government agent'.

This was Comrade Paschal Bafyau, a full-time career Secretary-General of Nigeria Union of Railwaymen (NUR). It is instructive to note that Bafyau had been a government nominee[45] to the Political Bureau set up by the IBB regime in 1986 to chart a political course for Nigeria. He was also a product of the National Institute for Policy and Strategic Studies (NIPSS) Kuru[46] which is widely regarded as a 'cult of power'[47] in Nigeria. It is hardly surprising therefore that under him the NLC became a weak-kneed organization that was always seeking compromise with the government. The anti-SAP nationwide demonstrations of 1989 and 1992, during his tenure, were masterminded by human rights and pro-democracy organizations in conjunction with some affiliate unions of the NLC. And on the annulment of the June 12 1993 Presidential election the NLC procrastinated until the Campaign for Democracy (CD) seized the initiative by masterminding a nationwide strike action to protest government action[48]. Thus, there was no vibrant and assertive apex labour organization that could champion the interest of the people.

The military regimes also manipulated ethno-religious factors to polarize the polity and lull the people into docile existence. In fact, through the unwarranted involvement of military rulers in religious matters in Nigeria, ethnicity and religion coalesced to become the bane of the society. Successive military governments since the Yakubu Gowon era patronized the two dominant religions (Islam and Christianity) as means of ensuring regional and federal control, the secular nature of the Nigerian state[49] notwithstanding. However, the level of patronage was subject to individual regime's perception of the extent to which it could go to acquire legitimacy and popularity. Thus, while some regimes covertly patronized one or both religion(s) on a pragmatic basis, others went all out to identify with and in fact gave state backing to a particular religion[50]. In both cases gov-

ernment patronage manifested in the establishment of Pilgrims' Welfare Boards; celebration of some state functions (e.g. Armed Forces Remembrance Week and Independence Anniversary celebrations) in Mosques and Churches; government recognition of religious holidays, importation of Rams and Turkeys during *Eid-el-Kabir* and Christmas celebrations respectively to augment local supply, membership of religious bodies (e.g. Organisation of Islamic Conference, OIC and the Islamic Development Bank, IDB); and, usage of government-owned media organizations for religious propaganda.

The most controversial of all the religious moves of the military in Nigeria was the OIC membership issue. The romance with OIC dates back to the Gowon era. In 1969 when the organization was being inaugurated an unofficial Nigerian delegation was in attendance. But, it was not accredited; it was only accorded observer status. In 1971 the Gowon regime accorded official recognition to Nigeria's observer status in the OIC[51]. This move was needed by that regime to placate the vociferous muslim zealots in the northern part of the country who had started to accuse the government of being pro-christians[52].

Successive military regimes maintained the innocuous observer status until 1986 when the IBB regime surreptitiously changed it to full-fledged membership. As Arthur Nzeribe has rightly observed, IBB needed such moves "to establish his credibility as both a northerner and an authentic Moslem"[53]. His pariah status[54] in the Hausa/Fulani dominated northern political enclave made it compelling for him to make a gesture of "reassurance of his religion and origin"[55] if he was to earn the much needed political leverage.

However, the christians did not take kindly to this move. The result was the escalation of religious crises in the country. Devotees of the favoured religion became arrogant and intolerant while the other contestant for government favour (i.e. the Christians) became more vocal and censorious. But this did not deter the IBB regime as it moved once again to reassure the muslim folks through the Nigerian Pilgrims' Commission

Decree 6 of February 1989. This decree was not only pro-Islam but also discriminatory against other religions. Section One of the Decree charged the commission "with responsibility for the general welfare of Nigerians undertaking a pilgrimage to el-Haji or el-Umra or both pilgrimages"[56]. And, as if to avoid ambiguity, section 15(2) specifically instructed that, "(In) the application of this decree, el-Haji has reference to the pilgrimage to the following places, that is, medina, Arafat and Muna"[57].

The Christian Association of Nigeria (CAN) contested this decree in the law court, but it lost on technical grounds. Decree 1 of 1984 had ousted the jurisdiction of law courts over government decrees. But, in his judgement, the presiding judge, Justice O. Silva, castigated the decree and exposed the sinister motive behind it. He observed that, "...Decree 6 is discriminatory and capable of causing disaffection where the desirable aims of peace and stability would be in jeopardy"[58]. Although the decree was later repealed and the functions of the defunct Nigerian Pilgrims' Commission were transferred to the Ministry of Internal Affairs, it had served the purpose of sending the right signals to the 'right people'. The overall impact of government dabbling into religious matter was the nurturing of disaffection and intolerance amongst the devotees of the different religions. This often led to serious crises that polarized and weakened the polity. For the military rulers, it augured well for a kind of 'divide and rule' tactics, reminiscent of our colonial past, and this enabled them to maintain a strong grip on the polity.

Closely related to the issue of religion was the factor of geo-ethnic patronage which manifested in the manipulation of some populist-oriented policies. These were the policies of 'quota system' and 'federal character'. Chapter II section 3 of the 1989 Nigerian constitution states that,

> The composition of the government of the Federation or any of its agencies and the conduct of its affairs shall be carried out in such manner as to reflect the federal character of Nigeria and the need to promote national unity, and also to command national loyalty

> thereby ensuring that there shall be no predominance
> of persons from a few States or from a few ethnic or
> other sectional groups in that government or in any
> of its agencies[59].

It is implicit from this constitutional provisions that certain
fears existed prior to the drafting of the constitution. Indeed, as
Adekunle Ajasin has rightly observed,

> The quota system and the federal character arrange-
> ment is the fear of the northern part of the country.
> Their fear is that the southern part has developed
> more than the north educationally, perhaps with
> western education...They also felt that to catch up
> with the south they should be given preference[60].

Although the quota system of selection or appointment was
intended to guarantee strict adherence to the principle of federal
character as means of achieving balanced representation of the
ethnic groups, there was manipulation such that merit was often
sacrificed and mediocrity enthroned in order to satisfy some
powerful ethnic configurations. In the implementation of the
policies, "geo-ethnic politics did not allow the dominant groups
in positions of power to consider other groups fairly and equi-
tably"[61]. This made the disadvantaged southern section of the
country to interpret "the principle to be a disregard to merit and
an attempt to hold a section down for others to catch up"[62].

Thus, instead of being integrative forces the policies widened
the gap and caused disaffection between the North (which the
policies favoured) and the marginalized South. Again, this contributed greatly to the weakening of the civil populace such that it
was not able to present a common front to challenge military dictatorship in good time. Those who were benefiting from such policies would naturally endorse the *status quo* overtly or covertly.

The military also patronized traditional rulers in order to
ensure that its interests were canvassed at the grassroots. This
was evident in the establishment of States' Councils of Traditional Rulers, inclusion of randomly selected rulers in federal
government delegations abroad, contract awards, extension of

government largesse and perquisites to some influential rulers. For instance, in 1991, the Military Governor of Niger State, Col. Lawan Gwadabe, donated new Mercedes Benz cars to Etsu Nupe, the Emirs of Agaie, Lapai, Minna, Suleija, Kontagora, Borgu and the Chief of Kagara. Col. Raji Rasaki of Lagos State emulated this gesture by extending similar largesse to the Obas of Lagos, Badagry, Epe, Ikorodu and Ikeja[63]. In addition, salaries and emoluments of traditional rulers were regularly reviewed upwards by different regimes even when those of civil servants remained stagnant. There was also the tacit encouragement of traditional rulers to intercede with the military government on behalf of estranged parties to it. The perennial students' anti-establishment protestations leading to government closure of educational institutions and the inevitable brushes with pro-democracy activists, politicians and even coup plotters, offered such opportunities. Some examples would serve to reinforce this observation.

In 1978 when Nigerian students protested violently against government hike in fees in tertiary institutions and in 1989 following the anti-SAP riots, the federal military government enlisted the assistance of traditional rulers in restoring the situation to normalcy[64]. Also in 1989, Chief Gani Fawehinmi, the irrepressible social crusader and human rights activist, was released from detention to the custody of the *Ooni* of Ife, Oba Okunade Sijuwade, who was expected to keep a check on him[65]. And, following the political problems created by the annulment of the June 12 1993 election, it took the intervention of the traditional rulers in the aggrieved south western part of Nigeria for the people to get involved once more in national political activities. For instance, on 21st May 1994 the traditional rulers held a meeting with Lt. Gen. Oladipo Diya, (the second in command in the new regime) at Ibadan. At its conclusion, the spokesman of the rulers, Oba Okunade Sijuade, called on Nigerians in general and the Yoruba in particular not to boycott the National Constitutional Conference elections slated for two days from then[66]. To a group that had been rendered almost irrelevant under modern political dispensations, these were opportunities that were eagerly

awaited, gratefully seized and maximally exploited. Thus, the military could always rely on the traditional rulers for support.

Furthermore, one other area in which the military used the politics of patronage to weaken the polity was the creation of states, local governments and boundary adjustments. As at independence Nigeria had only three regions (North, East and West). In 1963 the Mid-West region was carved out of the Western region to make the number four. The number of states was increased by military fiat to twelve in 1967 by the Yakubu Gowon regime. In 1976 the Mohammed regime increased the number further to nineteen. In 1987 it jumped to twenty-one and this was further increased to thirty in 1991 by the IBB regime. As at 1996 the figure had reached thirty-six. Also the number of local government councils went up progressively to keep pace with the state creation exercises.

It is important to note that with the exception of the 1963 exercise (which was a political gimmick for reducing the territories under opposition party control), all other state creation exercises were carried out by the military. It was relatively easy for the military to create states because of its authoritarian nature. The military capitalized on this attribute to induce subservience in the people. It is an incontrovertible fact that the military regimes in Nigeria actually encouraged people to demand for states by putting state creation on the transition programmes.

Thus, marginalized peoples (especially the minority elements) were encouraged to demand for states of their own. When such demands were met (wholly or partially) the military gained in popularity. And, even when they were not met the people were encouraged to wait for another opportunity. This development tacitly encouraged the endorsement of military rule which became synonymous with state creation. But the point that is often overlooked is that the balkanization of the polity implicit in the exercise was serving the purpose of weakening the position of the polyglot states vis-à-vis the center where the military grip was most profound.

Also, influential civil organizations, trade unions and institutions unofficially benefitted from government largesse as indirect

means of compromising them. For insance, between 1990 and 1992 more than N200 million was spent as extra-budgetary donations to such bodies by the IBB regime. Details of some of the donations are highlighted in the table below:

TABLE IV: Some of the Extra Budgetary Spending of the President Between 1990 And 1992 (In N Millions)

AMOUNT DONATED	PURPOSE	DATE
29.7	Special grant to alleviate the water problem at the University of Ibadan.	May 1990
1.0	To BCC Lions football club of Gboko for winning an African cup.	January 1991
10.0	To the Nigerian Bar Association (NBA)	March 1991
5.0	To Performing Musicians Association of Nigeria (PMAN)	February 1991
35.0	Towards the building of Arewa House in honour of Ahmadu Bello, the late Sardauna of Sokoto and the rallying figure of Northern politicians	August 1991
15.0	As grant to the Oyo State University of Technology	August 1991
5.0	To Nigerian Labour Congress (NLC) Endowment Fund	September 1991
25.0	To the building of Zik center in Zungeru.	November 1991
5.0	To Armed Forces Remembrance Appeal Fund.	January 1991
30.0	To Nigerian Union of Journalists' (NUJ) Media Foundation	October 1992.
10.0	To the building of NUJ Headquarters, Abuja	October 1992
5.0	To Nigerian Institute of Journalists' (NIJ) Endowment Fund	October 1992
13.0	To Nigerian Medical Association (NMA).	November 1992

Source: Collated from: *Tell*, 24th February 1992, P. 13; and Falola, Ajayi, Alao and Babawale ... pp. 99-100.

And, some relief packages in the form of marginal salary adjustments were sometimes approved for the working class (usually after protracted industrial actions or demonstrations like the anti-SAP riots of 1989 and 1992) ostensibly to cushion the effect of the hyper-inflationary conditions. In all cases the relief packages were not far-reaching enough to make any serious impact on peoples' living standard. The only exception would seem to be the 'Udoji award' of 1974/75.

It will be recalled that the Gowon regime in its attempt to bribe Nigerian workers and tacitly enlist their support for an extension of military rule, in 1974, ordered the payment of arrears for one year on the salary upward review recommended by the Jerome Udoji Commission. This move was totally out of tune with the observations contained in the Simeon Adebo Commission's report on a similar exercise in 1971. Rather than the payment of huge salary arrears on the recommended salary review the Adebo Commission felt that it would be more expedient to beef up social welfare programmes and bring down the cost of living[67].

Predictably, the hitherto highly marginalized workers who suddenly found themselves with large sums of money began to indulge in conspicuous consumption. The craze for imported goods became well established and the economy was put in jeopardy. Succeeding regimes made half-hearted attempts to rescue the economy through such superficial policies as 'low profile', 'austerity measures', 'counter-trade, and the Structural Adjustment Programme (SAP)[68] ;all of which created more distortions and ruined the economy. No serious attempt was made by any of the regimes to liberate the economy from the shackles of neo-colonial bondage and to introduce fundamental welfarist orientations that would have improved the lot of the people.

Rather, the gross mismanagement of the economy from the days of oil boom in the '70s up to the SAP – induced excruciating conditions in the 80s and 90s[69] served the purpose of further impoverishing the workers and masses thereby weakening their resistance to the military rulers. Whether this was deliberate or

incidental is a moot point. The incontrovertible point, as it has
been put elsewhere, is that:

> ... a poorly fed, badly housed, ill-educated (or not
> educated) and highly marginalized people cannot
> pitch itself against the might... of an army of occu-
> pation that our military organization has become.
> Under this situation people are easily cajoled, bribed,
> co-opted, blackmailed or compromised into legiti-
> mizing military oligarchy[70].

The quest for popular acceptance that would lead to the prolongation of military rule was not restricted to the domestic
environment. The federal military government spent large sums
of money (since the days of General Gowon) as grants or donations to decolonising or distressed African countries[71]. It was also
involved in funding, and participating directly in, multi-lateral
peace-keeping operations (like the Economic Community of
West African States' Monitoring Group's (ECOMOG) operations in Liberia) for the purpose of international acclaim thereby
diverting attention from domestic problems. We can recall that
Nigeria had been involved in a similar exercise in Congo in 1960
under the umbrella of the U.N. peace keeping force. But the level
of her involvement then was moderate and reasonable. Whereas
the ECOMOG operation was masterminded and almost unilaterally funded by Nigeria. She also had the largest number of
soldiers in the force[72].

In addition, large sums of money were regularly expended
for laundering the image of military regimes internationally. This
was especially so during the IBB and General Abacha eras. Public
relations outfits, influential individuals and diplomats were com-
missioned to carry out the assignment in Europe and America.
The essential purpose being the desire to create a supportive
international environment for the prolongation of military rule.
Although the military did not succeed in its international mission,
internally the politics of patronage and subordination yielded the
desired results of prolonging the life of some regimes.

IMPACT ON THE POLITY

As has been alluded to, the military governments, since the days of General Gowon, had unrestricted access to a progressively increasing national resource pool which they appropriated and distributed as they deemed fit. They could therefore afford to establish institutions, create opportunities and appointments for their civilian counterparts thereby giving the impression that the government was a form of diarchy involving both military and civilian personnel. But the military rulers only used this device to contain their influential civilian counterparts since they were usually coopted into government in subordinate positions. The real power and authority resided with the military oligarchy.

Geo-ethnic politics in Nigeria, especially the north-south rivalry also played into the hands of the military. Policies like quota system, federal character and the involvement of the military governments in religious matters were to the advantage of the predominantly muslim North. In fact, it would not be too far-fetched to assert that the military in Nigeria carried out a 'northern agenda' aimed at monopolizing political power by citizens of that region. The groundwork for this development could be said to have been laid shortly before and consolidated immediately after independence when northern politicians (especially the Premier of that region) actively encouraged their promising youth to join the army. We can recall that in July 1966 a counter coup masterminded by northern army officers terminated the six month old regime of General Ironsi. Also in 1983, when it was apparent that the inept Shehu Shagari administration would have to be forcefully removed, northern officers led by General Buhari quickly took advantage of the situation through coup d'etat.

And, in 1993, when it appeared as if power would shift to the south as a result of the brilliant electoral performance of Chief M.K.O Abiola , the Babangida regime annulled the election. It proceeded to put in place an unconstitutional political arrangement known as the Interim National Government (ING) headed by a southerner (Chief Ernest Shonekan) which from all intent and purposes was not designed to last. It lasted for barely

three months before a new regime headed by another northerner (General Sani Abacha) supplanted it. The point we are putting across here is that there was an inter-connection between sub-nationalism and military rule in Nigeria and this impacted negatively on the organic unity of the country. In fact by August 1993 the country was on the brink of disintegration with the articulate segment of the civil society in the southern half of the country calling for a Sovereign National Conference to suggest new directions for the beleaguered nation. But the politicians who had been at the receiving end of the patronage system sold out to the military.

The question that arises here is that; why did the southern politicians remain timid in the face of such blatant political intimidation and marginalisation? The cynicism among the masses, widespread poverty, ignorance, naivety and selfish pursuits, partially account for the complacent and often compromising posture of the southern politicians. Their self-seeking orientation – an attribute which made them either good losers or avaricious winners – made them to be easily susceptible to bribery and compromise. Thus, it was not uncommon for defeated or disgruntled politicians to be clamouring for the prolongation of military rule because they would not want to leave certainty (in terms of extant network of patronage and commercial connections) for uncertainty implicit in the 'winner-takes-all' political disposition in Nigeria.

It is within this context that we can understand the compromising attitude of a large segment of the civil populace towards the usurpers of political power. Reactions to the manipulation of the transition programme in 1993 (which shall be discussed more elaborately in chapter five) clearly epitomised the "if you cannot beat them ,join them" syndrome. In fact, the military would not have been able to get away with the annulment of that year's election but for the collusion of the political class[73]. From the foregoing it is not strange that Nigeria was saddled with a largely compromising political class and an apathetic civil populace that did not offer serious resistance to military rule in good

time. They were only roused from their lethargy when they got wise to Babangida's antics. But it should also be noted that the military had been employing repressive methods to militarize the polity in order to induce compliance. The method and instances of the attempts at militarisation form the subject of discussion in the next chapter.

Notes

1. Richard Sandbrook: "Patrons, Clients and Factions: New Dimensions of Conflict Analysis in Africa", in *Canadian Journal of Political Science*, 5(1) 1972, p. 119.

2. Richard A. Joseph: *Democracy and Prebendal Politics in Nigeria: The Rise and Fall of the Second Republic* (Ibadan: Spectrum Books Ltd., 1991) p. 73.

3. Ibid.

4. See, Akin Alao: "Military Rule and National Integration", in Toyin Falola (ed.): *Modern Nigeria: A Tribute to G.O. Olusanya*,(Lagos: Modelor, 1990) p. 129.

5. Ibid.

6. See, S.T. Akindele: "The Transition to Civil Rule Programme and the Role of Local Government in Enhancing Grassroots Representative Democracy", in S.G. Tyoden (ed.): *Transition to Civil Rule: The Journey So Far*, (Lagos: NPSA, 1992) p. 91.

7. See, J.'Bayo Adekanye: "The Military in the Transition", in Larry Diamond, *et al* (eds). *Transition Without End: Nigerian Politics and Civil Society Under Babangida* (Ibadan: Vantage Publishers, 1997) pp. 66-67.

8. Ibid, p. 67. For greater details, see, Adekanye: "Towards Explaining Civil-Military Instability in Contemporary Africa: A Comparative Political Mode", in *Current Research on Peace and Violence* 8(3x4) 1978, pp. 195-197; and "Pay, Promotion and Other Self-Regarding Interests of Military Intervention in Politics", in *Military Affairs* 45(i) 1981, pp. 18-22.

9. See, James, O. Ojiako: *13 Years of Military Rule, 1966-79* (Lagos: Daily Times Publication, 1979) p. 147.

10. See, *Tell*, 7 December 1998. p. 20.

11. Ojiako: 13 Years... p. 130.

12. Ibid.

13. See, *West Africa*, 12 October, 1987, p. 2048.
14. Bali tendered his resignation when he was reassigned to the Internal Affairs Ministry in a cabinet reschuffle. See, Adekanye, The Military, p. 60.
15. 'Langtang Mafia' is an oblique reference to some middle level and senior military officers of Langtang extraction who were very influential in military politics. For instance, the coup that brought Babangida to power was said to have been masterminded by the Langtang mafia whose most senior serving officer then was Lt. Gen. Domkat Bali
16. Adekanye: p. 61.
17. For a comprehensive compilation of the retirees list at this period, see, *Newswatch*, 17 September 1990, pp. 15-20.
18. See, *African Guardian*, 1 October 1990, pp. 12-18.
19. See, Adekanye: p. 61 and Adeolu Akande: "Machiavellian Statecraft, Corporatism and Neo Patrimonial Rule: Nigeria Under General Ibrahim Babangida" – Unpublished Ph.D Thesis, University of Ibadan, Ibadan, 1997 pp. 149-165
20. Akande: p. 149.
21. Adekanye: p. 61.
22. Ibid, pp. 61-62
23. See, *African Concord*, 26 March 1990, 'Cover Story'.
24. Adekanye: p. 63.
25. For details, see, *Tell*, 24 February 1992. pp. 10-15.
26. Akin Iwayemi: "The Military and the Economy", in O. Oyediran (ed.): Nigerian Government ... p. 62.
27. See, James Oluleye: *Military Leadership in Nigeria, 1966-79* (Ibadan: University Press, 1985) p. 157 and James Ojiako: *13 Years of Military Rule* (Lagos: Daily Times Publication, 1979) p. 83.
28. Adekanye: pp. 63 & 64.
29. Akande: p. 124.
30. Ibid.
31. I*bid.*
32. See, Chapter Two above
33. O. Olagunju, A. Jinadu and S. Oyovbaire: *Transition to Democracy in Nigeria (1985-1993)* (Ibadan: Spectrum Books Ltd.., 1993) Addendum C.

34. Ibid., Addendum D.

35. Ibid., Addendum E.

36. Kayode Soremekun: "The Military, the Colluding Elite and Democratisation in Nigeria" – paper presented at the National Conference on Corruption and Democratisation in Nigeria (1983-1993), University of Ibadan, 19th-20th September, 1995, p. 10.

37. Ibid.

38. See below, Chapter Four.

39. See, Ojiako: p. 94.

40. See, *African Concord*, October 19, 1992, pp. 37 and 38.

41. Hassan Adebayo Sunmonu: *Trade Unionism in Nigeria: Challenges for the 21st Century* (Lagos: Friedrich Ebert Foundation, 1996) p. 15.

42. F.U. Kaueven: "Trade Unions and National Security", (Mimeo, 1977) cited in A. Momoh: *Labour and Democratisation: Honest Brokerage or Collusion?* – Paper presented at the National Conference on Corruption and Democratisation in Nigeria (1983-1993), University of Ibadan 19-20 September 1995, p. 4.

43. Ibid., p. 8.

44. Ibid., p. 12.

45. See, *Report of the Political Bureau* (Abuja: MAMSER, 1978) pp. 6 & 7.

46. Momoh: p. 9.

47. See, *Newswatch*, November 27, 1989(Cover story).

48. See, *Nigerian Tribune*, July 6, 1993 pp. 1 & 2.

49. Chapter One, part II, Section 10 of the 1979 Nigerian Constitution affirmed this Secular status.

50. See, 'Gboyega Ajayi: "Government and Religious Patronage in Contemporary Nigeria (1980 – 1989): Implications for the Stability of the Nation", in *Zeitschrift Fur Afrikastudien* (ZAST) NR. 7/8, 1990, p. 56.

51. See, *African Guardian*, 18th June 1990, p. 21.

52. See, Y. B. Usman: *The Manipulation of Religion in Nigeria, 1977-1987* (Kaduna: Vanguard Printers Ltd., 1987) p. 84.

53. *African Guardian*, 3rd October 1988, p. 37.

54. IBB hails from Minna (Niger State) at the fringe of the erstwhile Sokoto Caliphate, the descendants of which still exert a lot of political influence in modern Nigeria

55. *This Week*, October 1988, p. 21.

56. *The Guardian*, 3rd March 1989, p. 1.

57. Ibid., p. 2.

58. See, *Vanguard*, 26th April 1989, p. 2.

59. See, Constitution of the Federal Republic of Nigeria (Promulgation Decree 1989), in Supplement to Official Gazette Extra ordinary no. 29. vol. 76, 3rd May 1989, p. A79.

60. See, *African Concord*, 5th October, 1992, p. 46.

61. Akin Alao: "Military Rule and National Integration" ... p. 136.

62. Ibid. p. 138.

63. See, *Tell*, 24 February 1992, pp. 14-15.

64. See, *Newswatch*, 13th November, 1989, p 27.

65. See, *African Guardian*, 30th October, 1989, p. 21.

66. See, Sunday Tribune, 22 May 1994, Pp.1, 10 and 11.

67. See, NAI/CE/A15B – Adebo, S.O. and 5 others: Second and Final report of the Wages and Salaries Review Commission together with the White Paper, 1970-71.

68. See, S. Adejumobi: "The Military as Economic Manager: The Babangida Regime and the Structural Adjustment Programme" – Unpublished Ph.D thesis, U.I. Ibadan, 1999.

69. For details on the dehumanizing results produced by SAP in Nigeria, see, Akin Fadahunsi, Adebayo Olukoshi, Abubakar Momoh and Tunde Babawale: "Nigeria Beyond Structural Adjustment: Towards a National Popular Alternative Development Strategy", in Akin Fadahunsi and T. Babawale (ed.): *Nigeria Beyond Structural Adjustment* (Lagos: Friedrich Ebert Foundation, 1996) pp. 35-42.

70. 'Gboyega Ajayi: "General Abacha's Transition Programme: What Prospects for the Future?" in Dipo Kolawole and Nazeem Mimiko(eds.) *Political Democratisation and Economic Deregulation in Nigeria under the Abacha Administration 1993-1998* (Ado-Ekiti: Department of Political Science OSUA, 1998) pp. 55-56.

71. See, Alaba Ogunsanwo: "Nigeria's Foreign Relations, 1970 – 1975", in *Nigerian Journal of International Affairs*, 4 (1 &2), 1978, pp. 39-41

72. For greater details, see the following: *Newswatch* September 10 1990, pp. 28-29; *Newswatch*, October 17 1990, p. 31; *Newswatch*, October 1 1990, pp. 30-31. *The News* April 29 1996, pp. 9-13 and *Sunday Sketch*, December 7, 1997, pp. 11 & 12.

73. For greater details, see, Somerekun: The Military, The Colluding Elite... pp. 13-14.

CHAPTER FOUR

THE MILITARISATION OF THE NIGERIAN POLITY

INTRODUCTION

From all indications, the underlying philosophy of military rule in Nigeria (especially since the conclusion of the civil war) was 'militarism'. This has been defined as,

> ... a doctrine or system that values and accords primacy in state and society to the armed forces. It exalts a function, the application of violence–and an institutional structure, the military establishment. It implies both a *policy* orientation and a *power* relationship (emphasis in the original)[1].

In Nigeria there was the deliberate extension of military ethos to politics and governance in order to ensure a kind of 'barrack- like' unquestioning obedience to constituted authority. It should be stated from the outset that the attempts to entrench military ethos in the Nigerian polity were either overt and consciously made or covert and innocuous. These shall be addressed in sequence.

OVERT MILITARISATION STRATEGIES

Right from the inception of military rule in Nigeria the trend has been to suspend some vital sections of the existing constitution and rule the nation by decrees. The most enduring of all the decrees was the State Security (Detention of Persons) Decree[2] which gained notoriety as 'Decree Two' under the Buhari and Babangida regimes. It was initially enacted and minimally utilized by the Ironsi regime. The Decree was variously known as

Decree 3,8 and 10 in its early days under the Ironsi regime. Essentially, the Decree "authorizes the arrest and detention of certain persons mentioned in schedule one of the decree in the interest of Nigeria". The decree was regularly reviewed by different regimes in order to give it more bite. In 1984 (under the Buhari dispensation) it attained its most dreaded form and was known ever since as 'Decree 2'. With the operation of this and other decrees, issues of human rights, rule of law, social justice and equity were held in abeyance. In fact, as successive regimes began to lose grip over the governance of the country, and in moments of desperation or in order not to lose face, the 'cutting edges' of old decrees were either sharpened or new ones were enacted. For instance, there was Decree 4 (the Protection of Public Officers Against False Accusations) of 1984[3] which replaced Decree 11 of 1976 and deliberately designed to deal with the Press which had by then become a thorn in the flesh of the military.

The decree stated that,

> Any person who publishes in any form, whether written or otherwise, any message, rumour, report or statement which is false in any material particular or which brings, or is calculated to bring, the Federal Military Government or the Government of a state or a public officer to ridicule or disrepute shall be guilty of an offence under this decree[4].

It went further to add that,

> (In) any prosecution for an offence under this Decree the burden of proving that the message, rumour, report or statement which is the subject matter of the charge is true in every material particular shall, notwithstanding anything to the contrary in any enactment or rule of law, lie on the person charged[5].

And that,

> Any person found guilty of an offence under this Decree shall be liable on conviction to be sentenced to imprisonment for a term not exceeding two years

without the option of a fine and, in the case of body corporate, to fine of not less than N10,000[6].

The tribunal could also order the Federal Military Government to confiscate the equipment of the offending media house[7]. And more importantly "(No) appeal shall lie from a decision of any tribunal established under this Decree"[8].

In order to demonstrate that the decree was not a mere 'paper tiger', two journalists (Messrs. Nduka Irabor and Tunde Thompson) and their employer (Guardian Newspaper) were soon made scapegoats. Their offence was publishing a list of ambassadorial postings without clearance from the appropriate quarters[9].

This move achieved the desired objective of checking the 'meddlesome' activities of the press (at least until the termination of the Buhari regime that sponsored the decree). There was also Decree 20 of 1984 which placed the death penalty on eleven offences some of which ordinarily ought not to attract more than a few years imprisonment. The offences were arson, tampering with oil pipeline, import or export of Mineral Oil or Ore with intent to defraud the Federal Military Government, dealing in cocaine, dealing in Petroleum products, armed robbery, counterfeit currency, treason, kidnapping, lynching and possession of arms and ammunitions[10]. All these engendered an atmosphere of fear and intimidation which conduced to authoritarianism.

Even under the IBB regime, which promised at its inception to accord respect to human rights and actually followed this up with the abrogation of Decree 4 and a review of Decree 20, the situation did not alter appreciably. We should expect this because the omnibus Decree 2 was retained and maximally utilized to silence opposition. In addition, more decrees were enacted to take care of virtually all aspects of national life[11].

It is important to note that although some of the decrees were draconian and retroactive (depending on the immediate purpose that they were meant to serve) yet they could not be contested in any law court because Decree 1 of 1984 had ousted the jurisdiction of civil courts over government decrees. To further compound the situation, military tribunals were regularly constituted

to adjudicate in matters that the ordinary law courts were meant to address. Apart from usurping the role of civil courts thereby subordinating them, the high-handed *modus operandi* of the tribunals turned them to highly dreaded government apparatuses. The threat of being exposed to any of them was enough to cowdown opposition to military rule. This state of affairs induced, in the civil populace, a kind of robotic obedience to, and grudging identification with, military oligarchies.

Moreover, the Police, Intelligence and Security apparatuses were regularly re-organized and their personnel paid higher salaries and other benefits to enhance their operations. They were also provided with newer and more sophisticated equipment for communication purposes. We can recall that the Nigerian Security Organisation (NSO), established by the Obasanjo administration shortly after the abortive coup of February 1976, was heavily utilized by the Buhari regime to police the civil society closely. As a result of its atrocious activities it put the government in bad light such that by the time Babangida took over the organization had to be reorganized and renamed. It was then split into three separate bodies known as; State Security Service (SSS) for intelligence within the country; Nigeria Intelligence Authority (NIA) for external intelligence, and Defence Intelligence Agency (DIA) for defence-related intelligence[12]. These complemented the already existing Directorate of Military Intelligence (DMI), to complete the intelligence network in the country. In addition, in 1989 the National Guard – a special elite corp – was put together for the purpose of detecting and breaking coups and for controlling public unrest and agitations[13].

Another important index of the deliberate attempt to turn Nigeria into a military state was the skewed nature of federalism under military tutelage. The center was made very strong and preponderant over the states either in terms of its control over the nation's resources (as noted previously) or the range of its political authority. Initially there was an attempt, through Decree 34 of 1966, to impose a unitary government over the multi-ethnic Nigerian State ostensibly to check centrifugal inclinations.

The arrangement under this decree was such that the former regions ceased to exist as before. They were now to be known as groups of provinces each of which would be subject to the military authority at the national level. Military governors would be appointed to oversee the group of provinces on behalf of the National Military Government. Also, the separate regional public services were to be merged and put under the umbrella of a National Public Service to be directed and controlled by a National Public Service Commission. Southerners stood to gain more from this new arrangement because of their relative educational advancement vis-à-vis their northern counterparts.

Therefore the Decree was very unpopular in the north and it was one of the factors that precipitated the counter-coup of 29th July 1966 led by northern officers. But what the Ironsi regime could not achieve through such a frontal assault on the *status quo* was achieved thereafter by subsequent military regimes, albeit, in a more suave manner. Akin Mabogunje got the picture right when he observed that,

> ...subsequent military-imposed constitutions have done more or less the same thing, (as Ironsi-ours) reducing the constituent states of our federation from their coordinate status with the federal government to one of feckless and pliant financial dependency on the latter[14].

He identified the pre-disposing conditions to this state of affairs as "the unified command structure of the military and the super-abundant revenue accruing to the federal government from petroleum products"[15].

To be sure, the military succeeded in sustaining the façade of federalism while in actual fact the arrangement was in the form of unitary government in which, "the states and their organs (are) no more than administrative units of the federal government"[16] instead of being loose components of the polity. This is to be expected because the military organization, "is a chain of command whose members are integrated in a strict relationship of subordination and superordination"[17]. It was this orientation

that was carried over to politics and governance. Col. Olagunsoye Oyinlola, one time military administrator of Lagos State, once remarked, in a personality interview, that, "(I) govern Lagos State as a military formation because it is the only experience I have"[18]. We must add that the situation at the federal level was the same.

This regimental process was assisted by the civil service which share certain fundamental attributes with the military. These have been identified as,

> ... functional specialization, role specificity, a hierarchical organization that is characterized by centralization, upward and downward communication flows and superior – subordinate relationship; order, discipline, internal cohesion and esprit de corps; secular rationality; and a commitment to goal achievement and to national service[19].

These attributes made the civil service to be amenable to the military agenda and this partly explains the close working relationship between the two institutions. Since the military lacked the necessary organizational and managerial skills with which to rule modern societies alone, it stands to reason therefore that it would seek alliance with 'like minds'[20].

Moreover, the civil service is believed to possess abundant technical expertise and managerial capability[21]. These attributes enabled it to secure vantage positions under military dispensations. For instance, under the Gowon regime we had the 'super' Permanent Secretaries who were much more influential in government circles than the political appointees (commissioners) who were supposed to be their bosses. In fact, they almost overshadowed the military rulers. It was the Mohammed regime that cut them down to size in two ways. First, the nation-wide purge of the civil service in 1975 saw many civil servants either retired or dismissed. Second, the permanent secretaries were barred from attending meetings of the SMC, the highest ruling body in the country. These moves affected the morale of the civil service severely[22] and induced in the 'surviving' officers a kind of inden-

tured servitude towards military rulers. Thus, what we have had since the reform was a pro-military civil service.

This manifested in an enthusiastic support for, and close working relationship with, military rulers by civil servants. The 'loyalty' of civil servants therefore served "ample notice on prospective coupists that, they could readily count on the support of the civil service, anytime the decision was made to disrupt the political life of the country"[23]. This disposition did not augur well for total military disengagement from politics. For as Stephen Olugbemi has rightly observed, "once in a position of power and influence, only very few may want to get out permanently"[24]. He went ahead to suggest that for a post-military civilian administration to survive in Nigeria, "the higher civil service must be debriefed of its assumed intrinsic right to political leadership"[25].

Unfortunately this re-acculturation process was not thoroughly executed in the various civil service reforms under the military. The result was the sustenance of a very powerful 'loyal constituency' for the military. Little wonder then that military regimes in Nigeria have been described as more or less 'military-civil service' coalition governments[26]. Although, the civil service is expected to be loyal to any government of the day and so could be said to be performing its traditional role under military regimes, its structure and orientation made it a more influential institution under the military.

Perhaps the most important index of the militarisation of the Nigerian polity in the period under consideration was the regular employment of coercive and repressive methods by the military to cow-down the citizenry. This manifested in two major ways. First, there was what could be referred to as the 'mad-dog syndrome' in civil-military relations in Nigeria. This could be described as, the different manifestations of the brazen use of force by the military on civilians either as reprisal for real or imagined grievances or for the purpose of outright intimidation.

It was a high ranking military officer and commandant of the Airforce Base at Ikeja, (Air Vice Marshal Nura Imam) who coined the term 'mad-dog' while commenting on the conduct of some Airforce ratings who had carried out a punitive expedition

against Chief M.K.O. Abiola and his household on 25th January 1988. A traffic accident involving one of Abiola's children and an Airforce driver led to the fracas[27].

However, it is important to note that similar incidents had always characterized civil-military relations in Nigeria since the inception of military rule. Some examples drawn across the country would serve to buttress this claim. In 1968 four journalists in the employment of the Western Nigerian Television W.N.T.V were brutalized by soldiers on the orders of the military governor (Brigadier Adeyinka Adebayo). They were alleged to have insulted his wife at a social engagement. One of them, Mr. Segun Sowemimo, died eventually from wounds sustained when they were being dealt with[28]. In 1974, another journalist, Minere Amakiri of the *Nigerian Observer*, was also brutalized on the orders of the Rivers State Military Governor, Commander Alfred Diete-Spiff, for having the temerity to file a story on the teachers' strike in the state the publication of which came up on the governor's birthday[29]. We can also recall the destruction of Fela Anikulapo's Kalakuta abode in Lagos, in 1977, by rampaging soldiers bent on teaching the musician a lesson for his anti-military postures[30].

Some other notable examples would include the Sogunle incident of 1983 when Airforce men destroyed twenty five cars and burnt two houses at the Ladipo estate in reaction to the alleged detention of some of their colleagues by 'vigilantes'[31]. In January 1988 alone there were three serious incidents. First, on 22nd January, soldiers burnt down seven vehicles and dealt ruthlessly with innocent passers-by at Oshodi, Lagos, because the wife of one of their colleagues was knocked down by a hit and run motorist while she was trying to cross the expressway[32]. Second, on the following day (23rd February) Naval men swooped on the Federal Housing Authority (FHA) estate at Ipaja, Lagos, in an attempt to prevent the eviction of their colleagues who were illegal residents in the estate. In the process FHA security office and the official residence of FHA securitymen were burnt[33].

The third incident which happened on the 25th was the raid on the Abiola household referred to earlier. One interesting

aspect of this particular incident was the report that the Airforce Base Commander, AVM Nura Iman, actually watched the preparation of his men for the raid without restraining them[0]. This action (or inaction) is suggestive of institutional support, or, at least, connivance.

The instances of military arbitrariness given above are mere random selection from several of such instances[34]. Therefore we are inclined to view the 'mad-dog syndrome' as a 'rapid response' military strategy for containing the civil populace (the members of which are derisively referred to as 'bloody civilians' in military circles). Apart from the fact that such conducts suggest disrespect for the due process of the law and social harmony, it also smacks of self aggrandizement and authoritarianism.

Second, radical civil organizations like the National Association of Nigeria Students (NANS), Academic Staff Union of (Nigerian) Universities (ASUU), Nigerian Medical Association (NMA), Nigerian Association of Resident Doctors (NARD), some privately-owned media organisations and the emergent Human Rights and pro-democracy groups, had their activities and influence curtailed through arrests and detention of their key members, proscriptions, blackmail, threats of elimination and other strong-arm measures[35]. All these destabilized, and so, moderated the influence of the perceived opposition groups in the polity.

All that we have discussed above fall within the scope of deliberate and overt attempts to turn Nigeria into a military state. However, there were also some other covert methods and policies which served the same purpose. The section below is devoted to the examination of such innocuous strategies.

COVERT MILITARISATION STRATEGIES

Over the years there was a proliferation of military institutions spread across the country. Examples of such institutions would include, Nigerian Military School, Zaria; Nigerian Defence Academy (NDA) Kaduna; Command and Staff College, Jaji; Training and Doctrine Command, (TRADOC) Minna; and, the National War College (NWC) Abuja. Some of the past

students of these institutions had occupied prominent political positions while the ones still there see themselves as potential office holders. These institutions have grown so much in stature that the average Nigerian family desires to have at least one of its siblings numbered among the intakes.

Primarily, these institutions were established to enhance the professional competence of military personnel. But they progressively became avenues for the politicization of military officers. For instance, the Nigerian Defence Academy (NDA) Kaduna was not only elevated to the status of a university, its curriculum was also expanded to take care of socio-political interests. Also, officers of the National War College were exposed to a curriculum of 70% military/strategic studies and 30% geo-politics (Nigeria and international)[36]. According to Lt. Gen. Jerry Useni, the first commandant of the college, the course would prepare officers to hold extra-regimental military and civilian appointments in national and international settings[37]. At the inception of the War College it was hoped that,

i)   the forces would be committed to a non-military intervention in the country's political and democratic process;

ii) (the forces) would develop an unalloyed loyalty to the Constitution of the Federal Republic of Nigeria; and,

iii) (the forces) would accept their subordination to democratically elected government[38].

But we are yet to witness positive results that could allay fears of the evolution of a military state.

In fact, instead of diverting the attention of the military officers from politics and governance, these institutions have only been preparing them (perhaps, unwittingly) to assume political responsibilities. This development is not lost on the civil populace many of whom started seeing careers in the military as stepping stones towards the realization of political ambitions. The posting of soldiers to secondary schools in 1978 to enforce discipline, the establishment of Command Secondary Schools, Navy and Airforce Secondary Schools across the country, the existence

of paramilitary organizations like Man O' War and Cadet in Colleges and Universities and the National Youth Service Corp (NYSC) initiated by the Gowon regime in 1973, continued to whet the youth's appetite for the military profession. And, for those who were past the recruitment age the next option was to identify closely with the military on social and political fronts. Therefore, in terms of orientation, affective attitudes and political disposition the tendency was towards militarism.

Thus, military ethos forcefully permeated the civil society. This could be seen in violent conducts, impatience and intolerant disposition, especially within the civil political class. In a communiqué released at the conclusion of the Conference on Constitutions and Federalism, put together by the Friedrich Ebert Foundation at the University of Lagos, in April 1996, it was rightly observed that,

> Prolonged military rule has ... affected the psyche of
> civilians and the political class such that they operate
> like the military thereby creating opportunities for
> the military's return to power[39].

For instance, it was not unusual to hear of civilian governors in the twilight days of the IBB regime dishing out instructions (in the military fashion) that must be obeyed with immediate effect. The long stay of the military in power and the mandatory observance of interest-serving practices like Armed Forces Remembrance Week, construction of cenotaphs of 'unknown soldiers' in state capitals and local government headquarters and the display of the portraits of incumbent military leaders in conspicuous public places assisted the acculturation process.

There were also attempts to broaden the scope of civil-military interface in two major ways. First, there was the fostering of civil institutions with strong political clout and whose 'students' cut across the civil and military population. The most striking example here is the National Institute of Policy and Strategic Studies (NIPSS) Kuru, Jos. This institution provided political education for military officers. Second, there was also the increasing involvement of retired military officers in politics and business (especially

the commanding heights of the economy – oil, banking, shipping, insurance etc). These shall be discussed one after the other.

NIPSS AND THE POLITICAL EDUCATION OF MILITARY OFFICERS

NIPSS was established by the General Obasanjo regime under Decree 20 of 1979,

> to provide a forum for initiators and executors of policy from all sectors of the economy to integrate the economy, promote harmony, communication, understanding and cooperation among participating organizations[40].

Randomly selected top civil servants, armed forces personnel, academics, labour leaders and nominees from the private sector have passed through the institution. But the admission ratio always weighted in favour of the armed forces and the police[41] despite the fact that it is not a military institution. The report of a study carried out by Syndicate One of the Senior Executive Course (SEC II),in June 1989, is very revealing. It states, in part, that,

> out of the 20 key positions in the entire Nigerian Army, 19 positions are held by the Institute's graduates. Similarly, in the Nigeria Police, all the first 20 key positions are manned by NIPSS graduates[42].

As at the time the report was compiled, an alumnus of the institution, Gen. Ibrahim Babangida, was the President and Commander-in-Chief of the Armed Forces[43].

The course content of the NIPSS covers six broad areas; policy and strategy; the domestic environment; regional studies; defence and security; international relations and international organizations; and, science and technology. In the various departments no formal classes are held. Rather, lectures are delivered by visiting lecturers from the universities and specialized institutions who are experts in the relevant fields. Seminars are also held for the students in groups under the supervision of directing staff. In addition the students undertake tours of some states of the country and some-

times visit some other African nations where they interact with top level personnel on important issues. With this kind of broad-based education and the calibre of people involved, the institute rapidly grew in stature to become a kind of 'think tank' for some regimes.

There is no doubting the fact that the institution wielded considerable influence in the nation's politics, especially during the Babangida era. For instance, it has been said that the postponement of the handing over of government to civilians from 1990 to 1992, the re-organisation of Nigeria's security network and the creation, by government, of the two political parties (the Social Democratic Party, SDP and National Republican Convention, NRC) that were imposed on the transition to civil rule programme in 1989, were initiated by the NIPSS[44]. In effect the NIPSS was an important institution which provided political education for military officers and served the interest of military rulers.

Military Moving into the Economy

From the mid-1980s there was a noticeable trend of retired military officers getting actively involved in politics. At the local government level, retired junior and middle level officers started making waves while their senior colleagues were competing with politicians at the state and federal levels. The examples of Generals Yar Adua, Gowon, Olutoye, Ogbemudia, Adebayo and Aduloju comes to mind here. In addition, Air Vice Marshal Shekari (rtd.) was once appointed the chairman of SDP caretaker committee[45]. Others who did not show direct interest in party politics were regularly appointed as Ministers, Director-Generals and Chairmen or members of the boards of corporations, banks and other business concerns in which the government had vested interests[46]. Some examples are, Generals Bajowa, Danjuma, Imam, Akinrinade, Suleiman, Bagudu, Shelleng, Maman, Magoro, Nwachukwu, AVM Omeruah and Group Captain Obakpolor. It can be argued that military men in Nigeria usually retire or are retired when they are still relatively young and in their prime, therefore they have to be actively engaged after retirement. But we must observe that they have been very selective in their choice of post-retirement careers.

According to the 1992 Annual Report of the Nigeria Deposit Insurance Corporation retired military officers had business interests in 24 out of 120 Merchant and Commercial banks in Nigeria; owned 13 Commercial and 7 Merchant banks outrightly; had controlling interests in 11 banks; and, had fronts in four other banks. The table below shows the banks, the retired officers involved and the positions occupied.

TABLE V: Retired Military Officers In The Nigerian Banking Sector (1992)

	BANKS	NAMES OF MILITARY OFFICERS	POSITION OCCUPIED
A. COMMERCIAL BANKS			
1.	Broad Bank of Nig. Ltd.	(a)Col. Sani Bello (rtd.) (b) Maj. Gen. Innih (rtd.) (c) AVM Usman Muazu (rtd.)	Chairman Director Director
2.	Chartered Bank Ltd.	Lt. Gen. M.I. Wushishi (rtd.)	Chairman
3.	Equitorial Trust Bank	Col. C.O. Ekundayo (rtd.)	Director
4.	Gamji Bank of Nigeria	Major M.H. Jokolo(rtd).	Director
5.	Gulf Bank of Nigeria	Maj. Gen. J.J. Oluleye (rtd.)	Director
6.	Habib Bank of Nigeria Ltd	Maj. Gen. Shehu Musa Yar' Adua (rtd.).	Chairman
7.	Highland Bank of Nigeria	AVM Ibrahim M. Alfa (rtd.)	Chairman
8.	Intercity Bank Ltd.	AVM John N. Yisa-Doko (rtd.)	Chairman
9.	North South Bank Ltd.	(a) General M. I. Wushishi (rtd.) (b) Air Comm Dan Suleiman (rtd.)	Director Chairman
10.	Trade Bank PLC	Maj. Gen. A. Mohammed (rtd.)	Chairman
11.	United Bank for Africa, PLC	Air. Comm. Samson Omeruah (rtd.)	Chairman
12.	Universal Trust Bank of Nigeria Ltd.	(a) Gen T.Y. Danjuma (rtd.) (b) Maj. Gen. Paul Tarfa (rtd.)	Chairman Director
B. MERCHANT BANKS			
13.	Continental Merchant Bank Nig. Ltd.	Col. Sani Bello (rtd.)	Chairman
14.	Great Merchant Bank Ltd.	Lt.Col. P.O. Ogbebor (rtd.)	Chairman
15.	Group Merchant Bank	AVM Mouktar Mohammed (rtd.)	Chairman
16	Int. Merchant Bank Nig. Ltd.	Maj. Gen. Mohammed Shuwa (rtd.)	Chairman
17	ICON Merchant Bank	(a) Maj. Gen. David Jemibewon (rtd.) (b) AVM. A.D. Bello (rtd.)	Vice Chairman Director

18.	Manufacturers' Merchant Bank	Maj. Gen. G.O. Ejiga (rtd.)	Director
19.	Nationwide Merchant Bank Ltd.	Lt. Col. Tunde Oyedele (rtd.)	Director
20.	Prime Merchant Bank	Maj. Gen. Hassan U. Katsina (rtd.)	Director
21.	Prudent Merchant Bank	Maj. Gen Z. Lekwot (rtd.)	Director
22.	Rims Merchant Bank Ltd.	Lt. Col. P.Z. Wyon (rtd.)	Director
23.	Royal Merchant Bank Ltd.	Maj. Gen. (Dr.) A. Rimi (rtd.)	Director
24.	Societe Bancaire Nig. Ltd. (Merchant Bankers)	(a) Gen. J.S. Jalo (rtd.) (b) Comm. O. Ebitu Ukiwe (rtd.)	Chairman Director

Source: Adapted from the 1992 Annual Reports of the Nigerian Deposit Insurance Corporation (NDIC) Published in *The News*, 24 January, 1994.

The example of Lt. Gen Danjuma (rtd.) is particularly striking. He was reputed to be on the board of several corporations, companies, banks and industries. His business profile is shown in the table below:

TABLE VI: The Danjuma Empire

S/N	COMPANY	SECTOR	POSITION OCCUPIED
1.	Nigeria – America Line	Shipping	Chairman
2.	Comet Shipping Agencies	Shipping	Chairman
3.	Universal Trust Bank	Banking	Chairman
4.	Union Dicon Salt	Industrial	Chairman
5.	Acres Farms, Takum	Agriculture	Chairman
6.	Oil Tec (Nig.) Ltd. Port-Harcourt	Energy	Chairman
7.	White Oil Company Kaduna	Energy	Chairman
8.	West Africa Milk Company	Dairy	Chairman
9.	Guinness (Nig.) PLC	Brewing	Chairman (till end of 1996)
10.	Tarabaro Fisheries	Fishing	Chairman
11.	T.Y. Chemicals	Industrial	Chairman
12.	World Trade African Forum	Service	Chairman
13.	Meridian Publishing Coy.	Publishing	Chairman
14.	Ideal Flour Mills	Industrial	Chairman
15	Eagle Flour Mills	Industrial	Chairman
16.	Nigerian Eagle Flour Mills	Industrial	Director
17.	SCOA (Nig.) PLC	Conglomerate	Ex-Director
18.	Agip. (Nig.) PLC	Energy	Ex-Director
19.	Nigeria Tobacco Company	Industrial	Ex-Director

Source: *Tempo*, 26th December 1996 (Cover Story) p. 3.

Some other retired officers had also acquired training, before or while in service, which fitted them into civil professions like Law, Medicine, Engineering, Farming, Accounting and Banking.

In these diverse ways, the interface of civil and military groups became much more extensive. More importantly the situation shows that the tentacles of the military had reached (directly or indirectly) virtually every sphere of national life in Nigeria. Kunle Amuwo aptly summed up the situation in the following words:

> over the years... the military's cultural and structural profile have so much permeated the political land- scape that today Nigeria is something close to a mili- tary state. Thus militarisation of politics, economy, industry business, commerce, indisciplined social activities of officers and men of the "disciplined forces", institutionalisation of armed terrorism etc. – all these elements loom large on the political horizon[47].

It is important to note that the militarisation of attitudes and social relations fostered a kind of regimental orientation. This created a supportive environment for the employment of other strategies of political power control (like the politics of patronage and subordination and the manipulation of the transition to civil rule programmes). Without doubt militarisation is antithetical to democratisation. In specific terms it constricts the democratic space through the restriction of freedom of speech, association, and the press.

Obviously this kind of situation was not conducive to democratization. It is therefore ironical that the military rulers could be claiming to 'democratise' the political process through the transition programmes. This only goes to show how deceitful the military rulers were. In fact, as it shall be demonstrated in the next chapter, the transition programmes were more or less cunning devices for the perpetuation of military rule in one form or the other.

Notes

1. "Militarism" in International Encyclopedia of the Social Sciences, 1968 ed., S.V.
2. See, J. Ojiako: *13 Years of Military Rule, 1966-79* (Lagos: Daily Times Publications, 1979) pp. 13-14.
3. See, *Federal Republic of Nigeria, Official Gazette*, Vol. 71. No. 18. April 4, 1984, pp. A53- A56.
4. Ibid., p. A53
5. Ibid.,p. A54.
6. Ibid. p. A55.
7. Ibid. p. A56.
8. Ibid.
9. See, *Newswatch* (Special Edition), January 20, 1986, p. 47.
10. See, Ibid., p. 48.
11. See, *Newswatch*, 12 November, 1990, pp. 17-18 and CDHR, *Human Rights Situation in Nigeria (Annual Reports for 1990, 1991, 1992 and 1993)* Lagos.
12. See, *The Guardian*, 6 June 1986, p. 1
13. See, *West Africa*, 22-28 July 1989 pp.12-13.
14. Akin Mabogunje: "On a Platter of Gold? Reflections on Four Decades of Governance" – 1997 Obafemi Awolowo Memorial Lecture reproduced in *Nigerian Tribune*, 6 May 1997, p. 19.
15. Ibid.,
16. Falola, Ajayi, Alao and Babawale: p. 160.
17. Claude. Ake: "The Significance of Military Rule", in *Proceedings of the National Conference on the Stability of the Third Republic* (Lagos: Concord Group, 1988) p. 120.
18. See,*Weekend Concord*, March 9, 1996, p. 6.
19. Stephen O. Olugbemi: "The Civil Service: An Outsider's View", in Oyeleye Oyediran (ed.): *Nigerian Government and Politics Under Military Rule* (Lagos: FFP Ltd., 1988) p. 99.
20. Ibid
21. Ibid. pp. 99-100.
22. See, p. Chiedo Asiodu: "The Civil Service: An Insider's View", in Oyeleye Oyediran (ed.): *Nigerian Government and Politics Under Military Rule* (Lagos: FFP. Ltd., 1988) p. 94.
23. Kayode Soremekun: *The Military, the Colluding Elite...* p. 8.

24. Olugbemi: p. 109.
25. Ibid.
26. Ibid. p. 98.
27. For more details, see, *Newswatch,* 8ᵗʰ February 1988, p. 2 and *African Concord,* 9ᵗʰ February 1988, p. 13.
28. See, Wole Soyinka: *The Man Died* (London: Rex Collings, 1972) pp. 13, 302 and 304.
29. See, Falola, Ajayi, Alao and Babawale: pp. 92-93.
30. For details of the incident and the legal proceedings, see 'Tunji Braithwaite: *The Jurisprudence of the Living Oracle* (Benin City: Ethiope Publishing Corporation, 1987) pp. 116-130, 214-249.
31. See, *African Guardian,* 11ᵗʰ February 1988, pp. 17-18.
32. See, *Newswatch*, 8ᵗʰ February 1998, p. 21.
33. See, African Concord, 9ᵗʰ February 1988, pp. 12-13.
34. For details of some other instances see the following: *African Guardian* 11ᵗʰ February 1988, p. 18; *African Concord*, 9ᵗʰ February 1988, pp. 12 and 13; *Newswatch* 8ᵗʰ February 1988, p. 21. And *Newswatch*, 22ⁿᵈ February 1988, pp. 13-16.
35. For details, see the following: Civil liberties Organisation (CLO): *Annual Reports on Human Rights in Nigeria* (various issues spanning 1987-1993); Ogaga Ifowodo: *Human Rights in Retreat: A Report on the Human Rights violations of the Military Regime of General Ibrahim Babangida* (Lagos: CLO, 1993); Committee for the Defence of Human Rights (CHDR): *Annual Reports* (1991-1993)' Victims – CDHR Newsletter; *Freedom Watch* – CDHR Monthly reports.
36. See, the Address of the Head of State and Commander-in-Chief of the Armed Forces, Gen. Ibrahim Babamgida, at the first Graduation ceremony of the National War College, reproduced in *Guardian*, 20 May 1993, p. 1.
37. See, *Newswatch*, 29 June 1992, p. 22.
38. Ibid.
39. *Constitutions and Federalism* (Lagos: Friedrich Ebert Foundation, 1996) p. 240.
40. See, *Newswatch*, 27 November 1989, p. 15.
41. Ibid., p. 17
42. Ibid. p. 15.
43. IBB belonged to the first set admitted in 1979. See, Ibid. p. 16.

44. Ibid. p. 17.

45. See, *Sunday Tribune*, 3rdJanuary1993, p. 7

46. See, J. 'Bayo Adekanye: *The Retired Military as Emergent Power Factor in Nigeria* (Ibadan: Heinemann Educational Books (Nigeria) PLC, 1999).

47. Kunle Amuwo: "The Nigerian Military as a New Class ..." p. 1.

CHAPTER FIVE

TRANSITION AS A STRATEGY

INTRODUCTION

The military promised to disengage from politics and handover government to civilians on three different occasions between 1966 and 1993. On one occasion, in 1979, the military actually handed the government to democratically elected civilians. But barely four years later, it returned to power. On another occasion, in 1993, there was a partial disengagement for barely three months before the military took over again.

Most military regimes in Nigeria, in their quest for legitimacy, usually came up with transition to civil rule programmes with a target date for handing over to elected civilian governments. But whether or not they were sincere about, and committed to, the programmes is a different matter altogether. However, the military rulers always conveyed the impression of being sincere but that the problem was with the civil political class. This, therefore, did not allow the transfer of power to be effected on a permanent basis. This chapter sets to prove that the perennial disengagement/transition programme was a ruse for perpetuating military rule in one form or the other.

In order to give room for fair analysis, a close examination of the content and direction of the transition programmes of the different regimes will be attempted. This will then be followed by general observations on the significance of transition programmes in reinforcing the military's grip on political power in Nigeria.

THE GRAND DECEIT: GOWON'S NINE-POINT
TRANSITION PROGRAMME (1970 – 1976)[1]

The General Ironsi regime at its inception in January 1966 promised to return the government to civilians as soon as possible. It actually went ahead to set up a Constitution Review Group[2]. But the July counter-coup which terminated its life did not allow the plan to be concretized. The Gowon regime that gained control of power also appeared to be favourably disposed towards a quick transfer of power but the outbreak of the civil war in 1967 delayed that plan until 1970 when the war ended.

The general feeling across the country in the immediate post-war period was for swift political transformation through the disengagement of the military from, and the civilianisation of, the political process. This mood appeared to have been well perceived by Gowon when he, in his national day broadcast to the nation on 1st October 1970, proposed a nine-point transition programme to be executed in six years. The programme was laid out in this order.

1. The re-organisation of the armed forces.
2. The implementation of the National Development Plan and the repair of the damage and neglect of the war.
3. The eradication of corruption in Nigeria's national life.
4. The settlement of the question of the creation of more states.
5. The preparation and adoption of a new constitution.
6. The introduction of a new formula for revenue allocation.
7. The conduct of a national population census.
8. The organization of genuinely national political parties.
9. The organization of elections in the states and at the center[3].

The target date for the completion of the exercise was to be 1st October 1976 when power would be handed over to an elected civilian government.

The programme was vague as there were no specific dates for the completion of any of the items listed therein. Also the time-frame set for the exercise was considered to be too long by

many people. This much was expressed in an editorial opinion of *West Africa*. It was observed that "there is no reason why General Gowon's nine tasks should not be completed well within the planned period"[4]. It went ahead to raise hopes by asserting that "(the) day may come when it will be asked whether the period might not be shortened in view of the progress made"[5]. But this was not to be as we will soon discover. However, Gowon was able to overcome this initial problem of credibility because the people decided to give him the benefit of the doubt. For, as Dare has rightly observed, "Gowon then enjoyed a large reserve of good-will and legitimacy from the humane way he handled the ending of the civil war and the post-war reconstruction efforts up to that point in time"[6].

However, Gowon squandered the peoples' goodwill through inaction and unnecessary footdragging in the implementation of the programme. The bloated armed forces was neither trimmed down nor reorganized as promised. The implementation of the Second National Development Plan and the repair of the damage and neglect of the war were advancing at an unhurried pace. There was no serious attempt on the part of the government to eradicate corruption. In fact, corrupt practices were tacitly encouraged by bureaucrats who stood to benefit thereby[7]. The only item that was concluded in the transition agenda was the national population census of 1973. And even the way and manner it was handled and the incredible results it produced, sowed the seed of distrust and heightened inter-ethnic tension. Instead of canceling the census returns (as its successor was to do later) the regime preferred to scuttle the whole transition programme.

In a national broadcast on the 1st of October 1974 (the 14th Anniversary of Nigeria's independence), Gowon declared the target date of October 1976 (still two years away) to be unrealistic. The broadcast did not proffer a new date, instead there was the vague promise that a panel would be set up "in due course ... to draw up a draft constitution, which when approved by the government will be referred to the people for adoption in a manner to be determined"[8]. There was also the promise "to broaden the

scope of civilian participation in the administration by setting up at Federal and State levels advisory councils comprising persons drawn from a cross section of the country"[9].

Without doubt, Gowon had been under pressure from anti-disengagement forces to have a rethink on the issue of handing over of power to civilians[10]. But there were also the pro-disengagement forces who kept on reminding Gowon that he should honour his pledge. However, "his personal inclinations against disengagement made him listen more to the anti-disengagement voices"[11]. The scuttling of the transition programme was neither patriotically motivated nor was it in the national interest. It was only in the interest of the Gowon regime. We wholeheartedly identify with the view that Gowon never really intended to honour the pledge to handover. He merely used the transition programme "to buy public support and time"[12]. This strategy was to be employed (albeit in a modified form) by the Gen. Babangida regime much later. But the Mohammed/Obasanjo regime that supplanted Gowon in office was under compulsion to initiate and prosecute a credible transition programme with minimum delay because Gowon's action had exposed the military to public odium.

MOHAMMED/OBASANJO'S FIVE-PHASE TRANSITION PROGRAMME, 1975-1979: MISSION ACCOMPLISHED?

The Mohammed/Obasanjo regime that seized power on 29 July 1975 apparently learnt some useful lessons from Gowon's misadventure given the promptitude with which its carefully crafted transition programme was evolved and executed. The following statements by General Obasanjo attests to this assertion:

> We appreciated that one of the things that brought a great credibility gap and loss of confidence in the military was the fact that Gowon reneged on his promise to hand over in 1976. If our administration as we saw it, was to redeem the credibility, the reputation and the confidence in Military, we had to bring in a Political Programme that would work and we had to pursue it undeterred and undiverted[13].

Thus, by the 1ˢᵗ of October, 1975 a five-phase transition programme was made public by General Muritala Mohammed in
his national day roadcast to the nation[14].The Programme which
was to be executed in four years was arranged as shown in the
table below:

**TABLE VII: Time Table of Military Return to Civil Rule in
Nigeria, (1975 – 1979).**

Phases	Programmes
Phase I	Creation and establishment of new states (August 1975 – April 1976); Constitution drafting (October 1975 – September 1976).
Phase II	Local Government re-organisation, reforms and elections; summoning of a Constituent Assembly to deliberate on the draft Constitution (September 1976 – October 1978)
Phase III	Electoral constituency delimitation; lifting of the ban on political party activities (October1978)
Phase IV	Holding of elections to legislative and executive offices at the state level.
Phase V	Holding of elections to legislative and executive offices at the Federal level; and handover of power by 1ˢᵗ October, 1979.

Source: J. Bayo Adekson: "Dilemma of Military Disengagement", in
Oyeleye Oyediran (ed.): *Nigerian Government and Politics Under
Military Rule, 1966 – 79* (Lagos; Friends Foundations Publishers
Ltd:, 1988) p. 220.

One glaring difference between this programme and that
of Gowon is that there were specific dates for the completion of
each item on the programme. Thus, the sincerity of the sponsors
was not in doubt and this went a long way in conferring credibility on the programme[15].

The scrupulously religious manner in which the programme
was executed was an added boost to the newly refurbished image
of the military. It will be recalled that on October 4, 1975 a
50 -man[16] Constitution Drafting Committee (CDC) was set
up under the chairmanship of Chief Rotimi Williams – a well
respected legal luminary. The other members of the committee

are: Chief Obafemi Awolowo, leader of opposition in the government of the first republic; Alhaji Aminu Kano, Chief Whip in the parliament of the first republic; Dr. Pius Okigbo, former economic adviser to the federal government and Ambassador to the European Economic Community; Alhaji Nuhu Bamali, former federal minister; Mr. Richard Akinjide, former federal minister; Dr. Kingsley Ozumba Mbadiwe, former federal minister.

Some of the others are Alhaji Sule Gaya, minister in the Northern Region; Alhaji A.G.F. Rasaq, former ambassador and legal adviser to the banned Northern Peoples' Congress; Dr A.Y. Aliyu, lecturer, Ahmadu Bello University, Zaria; Dr. Christopher Abashiya, Polytechnic Kaduna; Professor Sam. Aluko, Economist, University of Ife; Dr. Tam. David-west, lecturer, University of Ibadan; Mr Mamman Ali Makele, Senior Assistant Registrar, University of Lagos; Professor B. Nwabueze, University of Nigeria, Nzukka; Mr. Sam. Ikoku, an economist; Mr. Bola Ige, legal practitioner; Mr. M.S. Angulu, registrar, Ahmadu Bello University, Zaria; Professor E.U. Emovon, University of Benin and Mr. Rasheed Gbadamosi, playwright and former Commissioner in Lagos State.

Others are: Alhaji 'Femi Okunnu, former Federal Commissioner; Alhaji Buba Ardo, Attorney-General, North-Eastern State; Dr. I. Ahmed; Dr. Yusuf Usman, historian, Ahmadu Bello University, Zaria; Dr. Obi Wali, former Commissioner, Rivers State; Alhaji Shehu Malami, businessmen; Dr. E. Edozie, economist, University of Ibadan; Mr. Kanmi Ishola – Osobu, legal practitioner; Mr. David Dimka, Chairman, Benue-Plateau Television; Mr. P. Belabo, legal practitioner; Mr. Ekanem-Ita, University administrator; Chief I.I. Murphy, former parliamentarian; Alhaji S.M. Liberty; Dr. Kole Abayomi; Dr. O. Idris; Dr. U.O. Eleazu and Professor Billy J. Dudley, political scientist, University of Ibadan.

The others are: Dr. G.A. Odenigwe; Dr. O. Oyediran, political scientist; Mr. Paul Unongo; Alhaji Mamman Daura, Managing Director, New Nigeria Newspapers; Mr. Ibrahim Tahir; Dr. V. Diejemoah, economist, University of Lagos; Alhaji Ibrahim

Iman, politician; Dr. S. Aleyideno, Dr. Segun Osoba, historian, University of Ife; Alhaji Armed Talib, Chairman, Northern Nigerian Development Corporation; Dr. O. Ikime, historian, University of Ibadan; Alhaji Mamud Tukur, Institute of Administration, Zaria; and Mosignor Pedro Martins, Army chaplain[17].

As could be seen from the composition of the committee, the membership was drawn from the bar, private sector, universities, local government, former politicians and the military. On the 18th of October1975, the head of state, Brigadier Murtala Mohammed inaugurated the committee formally. In his speech at the occasion he pointedly recommended an executive presidential system of government for the country[18]. This precluded the consideration of other systems of government. The committee worked for about eleven months before coming up with a draft constitution which was submitted to the new head of state[19], Lt. Gen. O. Obasanjo, on 14th of September 1976. Two members of the Committee, Drs. O. Osoba and Yusuf Bala Usman (both historians) submitted a separate report to the political division of the cabinet office. However, it was the report submitted by the chairman of the committee that was thrown up for public debate and for the consideration of the Constituent Assembly (CA) established for that purpose.

The CA was made up of 203 elected and 27 nominated members. It began sitting in Lagos on 6 October 1977 and debated the draft constitution for about eleven months. Its recommendations[20] were presented to Gen. Obasanjo on 29 August 1978 and it was formally dissolved on September 20, 1978. The following day; i.e. 21st September 1978 the head of state signed Decree 25 which promulgated the new constitution into law. It was to be referred to as "The Constitution of the Federal Republic of Nigeria 1979" and would come into effect on October 1 1979[21]. Later that day, in a national broadcast, the head of state announced that seventeen amendments have been made to the constitution by the Supreme Military Council[22]. Some existing decrees were incorporated into the constitution. These were the National Youth Service Decree, Public Complaints Decree,

National Security Organisation and Land Use Decrees[23]. Obviously this was intended to ensure some measure of continuity.

In the same broadcast speech the ban on political activities, in place since 1966, was lifted. This was a far-reaching step towards disengagement. Before now some practical steps towards disengagement had been taken. For instance on 24 July 1978 the military governors in the nineteen states were redeployed and in their place military administrators were appointed. General Obasanjo explained that the removal of the military governors was to facilitate the "gradual disengagement of the military psychologically from the business of government"[24]. Furthermore, all military officers holding political appointments after July 24 1978 would not be re-integrated into the armed forces after October 1979[25]. Four Federal Commissioners – Brigadier J.N. Garba (External Affairs); Col. Mohammed Magoro (Transport) Col. M. Buhari (Petroleum) and Col. A.A. Ali (Education) were to return to military duties as from July 24, 1978. Also, Maj. General Henry Adefope (Labour) and Major General Mohammed Shuwa (Trade) were to retire with the commencement of civilian rule on 1st October, 1979. In addition Gen. Obasanjo (the Head of State) and Brigadier Shehu Yar Adua (the Chief of Staff, Supreme Headquarters) were to retire on the same day[26].

These developments portrayed the seriousness which the regime attached to the disengagement programme. But the most exciting development as far as the politicians were concerned was the lifting of the ban on political activities after twelve years. Thus, officially political associates could now gather openly. Without doubt, ban or no ban some form of political activities had been going on clandestinely. The speed with which political parties emerged shortly after the lifting of the ban attests to this. For instance, within 24 hours of the pronouncement two political parties had emerged. These were the Unity Party of Nigeria (UPN) and Nigerian Peoples' Party (NPP) whose birth was announced by Alhaji Waziri Ibrahim[27].

By 28 September- one week after the lifting of the ban – three other political parties had emerged. These were the National

Party of Nigeria (NPN), Nigeria Advance Party (NAP) and the Nigerian National Congress (NNC)[28]. The Peoples Redemption Party (PRP) and the Great Nigerian Peoples' Party (GNPP) – a splinter group of the NPP – were to come shortly thereafter.

Politicking started earnestly and elections into the Senate, House of Representatives, State Legislative Assemblies and Gubernatorial positions were held, as scheduled on, 7, 14, 21 and 28 July, 1979 respectively[29]. On August 11, 1979, the presidential election was held and on August 17, 1979, the Federal Electoral Commission (FEDECO) declared Alhaji Shehu Shagari of the NPN the winner. He was said to have "satisfied the provision of section 34 (A), subsection (1)(C)(1) of the Electoral Decree No.73 of 1977 by scoring the highest number of votes cast at the election"[30]. He also "satisfied the provision of subsection (1) (C) (11) of the same section. He has not less than one-quarter of the votes cast at the election in each of at least two-thirds of all the states in the Federation"[31].

The returning officer, Mr. Frederick Menkiti, explained further that "(the) Electoral Commission considers that in the absence of any legal explanation of guidance in the Electoral Decree it has no alternative than to give the phrase at least two thirds of all the states in the Federation – in Section 34(A) sub-section (1)(C)(II) of the Electoral Decree the ordinary meaning which applied to it"[32]. And that "(In) the circumstances, the candidate who scores at least one-quarter of the votes cast in 12 states and one-quarter of two-thirds, that is, at least one-sixth of the votes cast in the 13th state satisfies the requirement of the subsection"[33]. Reproduced below is the breakdown of the results of the presidential election as put together by FEDECO.

TABLE VIII: Federal Electoral Commission Computation Of Electoral Results Of The Presidential Election

STATES	TOTAL VOTES CAST	ALHAJI IBRAHIM		CHIEF AWOLOWO		ALHAJI SHAGARI		ALHAJI A. KANO		DR. AZIKWE	
		VOTES	%	VOTES	%	VOTES	%	VOTES	%	VOTES	%
ANAMBRA	1,209,039	20,228	1.67	9,063	0.75	163,164	13.50	14,560	1.20	100,083	82.83
BAUCHI	998,683	154,215	15.44	29,960	3.00	623,989	62.45	143,202	14.34	47,314	4.72
BENDEL	669,511	8,242	1.23	356,381	53.23	242,320	36.19	4,939	0.73	57,629	5.60
BENUE	538,879	42,993	7.89	13,864	2.57	411,648	76.37	7,277	1.35	63,077	11.71
BORNO	710,968	384,278	54.04	23,885	3.35	246,778	34.71	46,385	6.52	9,842	1.35
CROSS RIVER	661,103	10,105	15.14	77,775	11.76	425,815	64.40	6,737	1.01	50,671	7.66
GONGOLA	639,138	217,814	34.09	138,561	21.67	227,057	35.52	27,750	4.31	27,556	4.35
IMO	1,153,355	34,616	3.00	7,335	0.64	101,516	8.80	10,252	0.89	999,636	86.68
KADUNA	1,382,712	190,936	13.80	92,382	6.68	596,302	43.12	437,771	31.66	65,321	4.71
KANO	1,220,763	18,482	1.54	14,973	1.23	243,423	19.94	932,803	76.41	11,082	0.91
KWARA	354,605	20,251	5.71	140,006	39.48	190,142	53.62	2,376	0.67	1,830	0.52
LAGOS	828,414	3,943	0.48	681,762	82.30	59,515	7.18	3,874	0.47	79,320	9.57
NIGER	383,347	63,278	11.50	14,155	3.69	287,072	72.88	4,555	3.79	4,282	1.11
OGUN	744,668	3,974	0.53	689,655	92.61	46,358	6.23	2,338	0.31	21,343	0.32
ONDO	1,369,849	3,561	0.26	1,294,666	94.50	57,361	4.19	2,509	0.5	11,752	0.86
OYO	1,396,547	8,029	0.57	1,197,983	85.78	177,999	12.75	4,804	0.32	7,732	0.55
PLATEAU	548,405	37,400	6.82	29,029	5.29	190,458	34.73	21,852	3.98	269,666	49.17
RIVERS	687,951	15,025	2.18	71,114	10.33	499,846	72.65	3,212	0.46	98,754	2.35
SOKOTO	1,348,697	359,021	26.61	34,102	2.52	898,094	66.58	44,977	3.33	12,503	0.92
TOTAL	16,846,633	1,686,489		4,916,651		5,688,587		1,732,113		2,822,523	

Source: NAI/PX/G7F: The General Elections 1979 – Report by FEDECO.

At this juncture we consider it appropriate to make some observations about the way and manner power was handed over to Alhaji Shehu Shagari of the NPN. Of particular interest to us was the controversial interpretation of two-thirds of nineteen states to mean twelve two-thirds states instead of the general understanding and the previous practice of taking it to mean thirteen states in the elections preceding that of the president. It will be recalled that Chief Richard Akinjide of the National Party of Nigeria (NPN) first interpreted the electoral law to mean 12 states and one-sixth of the thirteenth state in a Television Network programme on 15 August 1979. Eventually it was this interpretation that FEDECO relied upon, two days later, in determining the winner.

Instead of falling back on the option of allowing the Electoral College to determine the winner as provided for in the electoral law[34], FEDECO went ahead to announce Alhaji Shehu Shagari as the duly elected president. The four other parties (NPP, UPN, PRP and GNPP) that presented candidates for the election promptly rejected FEDECO's declaration. Chief Obafemi Awolowo of the UPN (who came second in the election) went further to initiate legal proceedings, but all to no avail. The Election Tribunal first upheld FEDECO's decision and before Awolowo's appeal got to the Supreme Court, a new Chief Justice, Justice Atanda Fatai Williams, was appointed to handle the case[35]. Predictably, the decision was validated by the Supreme Court in a landmark judgement which the newly appointed Chief Justice said would not be cited as precedent[36].

It is also important to note that on the eve of Gen. Obasanjo's departure from office (when the deed had been done) the electoral provision was re-interpreted to mean thirteen states[37]. According to General Obasanjo, the amendment became necessary because "the SMC was convinced that the provisions requiring election by Electoral College were fraught with grave dangers and were unacceptable to the generality of the people"[38]. All these bastardized the electoral process by formalizing underhand tricks. It, however, ensured that power did not elude the favoured fraction

of the political class. The situation was succinctly captured by
Leo Dare in the following words:

> ...it could be seen that the Obasanjo regime manipu-
> lated the electoral system to install a regime it had
> linkages with,and a regime which during the election-
> eering campaign,promised not to probe the activities
> of the departing military government[39].

This development had serious implications for the Second Republic. In fact, it is hardly surprising that it lasted for up to four years.
To be sure, the ills of the First Republic were re-enacted in more
damaging forms[40], so much so that the masses once again became
disenchanted and restive. More importantly the determination
of the inept Shagari administration to remain in power at all cost
(especially through manipulations and electoral malpractices)
prepared the ground for the return of the military. Having tasted
power for thirteen years previously the restive military needed
very little excuse to seize political power once more. In other
words the factor of the lure of office was equally potent. But it
was the embarrassing outcome of the Second Republic, which
had portrayed the civilian politicians as inept, selfish and unpa-
triotic in the eyes of the generality of the people, that provided
the excuse for the take over.

The contention in military circle was that the politicians did
not learn any lesson from the previous failed attempts at democratic rule. It is, therefore, not surprising that the Gen. Mohammed Buhari regime which supplanted Shagari in office did not
come forth with any disengagement/transition programme. It
mistook Nigerians' disenchantment with the politicians of the
Second Republic and their enthusiastic welcome of the coup
as indications of a preference for military rule. Whereas, as we
have observed previously public opinion in Nigeria has always
regarded military rule as an aberration or at best a short-term
expediency to be tolerated before a democratic civilian government is put in place[41]. This was lost on the Buhari regime which
was set to rule *ad infinitum* and with iron hands.A fraction of
the military led by Gen. Ibrahim Babangida, the Chief of Army

Staff, capitalized on the growing unpopularity of the regime to execute a palace coup on 27 August 1985. The Babangida regime affected the posture of an 'arbitrator' and followed "historical necessity"[42] by pledging to handover power to civilians soonest while it actually harboured a hidden agenda for perpetuation in office. This will be substantiated in the section below.

TRANSITION WITHOUT END: IBRAHIM BABANGIDA'S POLITICAL TRANSITION PROGRAMME (1987 –1993)

On the assumption of office, IBB made it clear through policy statements, press interviews and releases that the regime would embark on a disengagement and democratization programme. The programme had a two-pronged approach – the economic and the socio-political processes. In his 1991 budget speech IBB articulated the processes in the following words:

> ... the reform package of this administration is constructed on two pillars. The first is on the economy which some have seen as being concretized in SAP. The second is the political programme which we have articulated in the Transition to Civil Rule Programme. These two elements are mutually reinforcing and both must be faithfully implemented[43].

It will be recalled that the IBB regime, in its early days, sponsored a national debate on whether or not it should take an IMF loan to which some stringent conditionalities were attached. Quite expectedly, the public demanded the rejection of the loan because it had all the trappings of neo-colonial bondage. The government gave the impression of yielding to public opinion by rejecting the loan. It, however, went ahead to initiate a facsimile of the IMF prescription in the form of a Structural Adjustment Programme (SAP)[44] under very harsh and dehumanizing conditions. The result was the rapid transformation of the nation into a debtor and beggar state and the pauperization of the citizenry (exempting few members of the ruling class and their clients). The gross inequalities that this programme engendered were to

disempower the less privileged masses thereby marginalizing them in the process[45].

It will also be recalled that on the 13th of January 1986, a seventeen – man Political Bureau was inaugurated by IBB and it was given the following terms of reference:

(a) Review Nigeria's political history and identify the basic problems which have led to our failure in the past and suggest ways of resolving and coping with these problems;

(b) Identify a basic philosophy of government which will determine goals and serve as a guide to the activities of government;

(c) Collect relevant information and data for the Government as well as identify other political problems that may arise from the debate;

(d) Gather, collate and evaluate the contributions of Nigerians to the search for a viable political future and provide guidelines for the attainment of the consensus objectives;

(e) Deliberate on other political problems as may be referred to it from time to time[46].

The Bureau discharged its duties conscientiously and came up with some far-reaching recommendations, the most important of which was that,

> Socio-economic power should be democratized through political and economic participation in all structures and organizations of power. The economy should be restructured largely along the socialist pattern with emphasis on self-reliance and social justice. Leadership should derive directly from the masses of the people in consonance with the ideology and philosophy of socialism[47].

It would have been a very auspicious beginning for a thorough-going democratization process if the government had accepted this recommendation. But it was rejected on the ground that "the principles enshrined in the 1979 constitution contained ideas that could form a philosophy for any progressive government"[48] without

recourse to any ideological label. Obviously the regime was better
disposed to the elitist liberal democracy which is too timid (given
the objective realities of the Nigerian state) to check military van-
guardism. Thus, the political transition programme as announced
in July 1987 was based on the presidential system of government
patterned along the U.S. model. It was laid out in this form:

Time Table for the Political Programme

3rd Quarter - 1987:
Establishment of the Directorate of Social Mobilisation
Establishment of a National Electoral Commission
Establishment of a Constitution Drafting Committee

4ᵗʰ Quarter - 1987:
Elections into the Local Governments on Non-Party basis.

1ˢᵗ Quarter - 1988:
Establishment of National Population Commission
Establishment of Code of Conduct Bureau.
Establishment of Code of Conduct Tribunal.
Establishment of Constituent Assembly.
Inauguration of National Revenue Mobilisation Commission

2ⁿᵈ Quarter - 1988:
Termination of Structural Adjustment Programme (SAP).

3ᴿᴰ Quarter - 1988:
Consolidation of gains of Structural Adjustment Programme (SAP).

1ˢᵀ Quarter - 1989:
Promulgation of a new constitution. Release of New Fiscal
    arrangements.

2ⁿᵈ Quarter - 1989:
Lift of ban on Party Politics.

3rd Quarter - 1989:
Announcement of two recognized / registered political parties.

4th Quarter - 1989:
Election into Local Governments on Political Party basis.

1st and 2nd Quarters – 1990:
Election into State Legislature and State Executives.

3rd Quarter – 1990:
Convening of State Legislatures.

4th Quarter – 1990:
Swearing –in of State Executives.

1st, 2nd and 3rd Quarters – 1991:
Census.

4th Quarter – 1991:
Local Government Elections.

1st and 2nd Quarters – 1992:
Elections into Federal Legislatures and convening of National
Assembly.

3rd and 4th Quarters – 1992:
Presidential Elections.
Swearing-in of new President and final disengagement by the
Armed Forces[49].

The programme was later elongated to August 1993 as we shall
see later.

Without doubt the programme was the most comprehensive
transition programme designed by any military regime during the
period of our study. It has been described as "a bold experiment
in political and cultural engineering"[50]. The informing sensibil-

ity in the drafting of the transition programme was that previous programmes were hastily put together and hurriedly executed and this was why civilian rule did not endure. Therefore the IBB regime favoured a gradualist approach. IBB's address to the nation at the launching of the programme subscribed to this view. He remarked that,"(As) you can see from the political programme it is aimed at establishing a gradual and graduated learning political process while establishing a new political order"[51]. This prepared the ground for the almost interminable transition programme that was foisted on the nation by this regime.

However, like other transition programmes before it, it over-emphasised structures, institutions and procedures without improving the lot of the people around whom the whole concept of democracy revolves. Even if the definition of democracy as "the government of the people, by the people, for the people" is considered anachronistic, the useful inference one can draw from it is that democracy is people-centred. Furthermore, the programme was not conscientiously implemented as could be seen in the constant tinkering with the time table[52], inconsistencies, manipulations, deliberate imposition of a disenabling socio-economic environment and lack of sincerity and commitment by the sponsor. These shall be validated presently. At the outset, some categories of people (old breed politicians, civil servants, armed forces personnel, convicts and ex-convicts) were banned from taking part in the exercise. Some of these people, especially the - 'old breed' politicians were later unbanned only to be banned again.

In a nationwide broadcast on 27 July 1986 Gen. Babangida announced the AFRC'S decision to ban all Second Republic politicians from participating in the transition programme[53]. On 23 July 1987 the ban was extended to cover all civilians who served in the First and Second Republics as well as military and police officers who have been convicted for abuse of office by a court or tribunal in any part of the country[54]. The ban was further extended on 29 March 1989 to include officials of MAMSER at federal and state levels; the National Electoral Commission (NEC); the National Population Commission (NPC); the Code of Conduct

Bureau; the National Revenue Mobilisation Commission and the Directorate of Food, Roads and Rural Infrastructure (DIFRRI)[55]. The Participation in Politics and Elections (Prohibitions) Decree 25 of 1987 and Decree 9 of 1989, which amended it in order to rope-in more people, gave legal backing to the government move. Whoever contravenes the decree was liable to a maximum fine of N250,000 or five years jail term or both[56].

On the 2nd and 3rd December 1991 thirteen banned 'old-breed' politicians were arrested for allegedly sponsoring newbreed politicians for the gubernatorial primaries held on October 19, 1991[57]. The indicted 'godfathers' and the persons and/or organizations which they allegedly sponsored are listed below:

TABLE IX: List of Banned Politicians and Their Proteges.

Accused	Party	Person Allegedly Sponsored	State
Abubakar Rimi	SDP	Sule Lamido	Jigawa
Olusola Saraki	SDP	Shaba Lafiaji	Kwara
Francis Arthur Nzeribe	SDP	Fabian Osuji	Imo
Bello Maitama Yusuf	NRC	Kabiru Gaya	Kano
Lamidi Adedibu	SDP	Kolapo Ishola	Oyo
Lateef Jakande	SDP	Femi Agbalajobi	Lagos
Christian Onoh	NRC	Sponsored NRC for the local government and governorship elections.	Enugu
Shehu Musa Yar'Adua	SDP	Funding SDP local government and governorship elections	Katsina
Solomon Lar	SDP	Fidelis Tapgun	Plateau
Jim Nwobodo	SDP	Gbazuagu N. Gbazuagu	Enugu
Bola Ige	SDP	Kolapo Ishola	Oyo
Paul Unongo	SDP	Moses Adasu	Benue
Lawal Kaita	NRC	Sponsoring NRC for the local government and governorship primaries/elections	Katsina

Source: Collated from *Newswatch*, December 16, 1991, Pp. 33-34.

It will be recalled that earlier, on 25 November 1991, twelve new-breed governorship aspirants had been disqualified and the

primaries in nine states quashed because of the unwholesome influence of the soon-to- be arrested politicians[58]. This prepared the ground for their arrest and prosecution.

On December 3 1991 some of the arrested politicians were arraigned before the Justice Fred Anyaegbunam Tribunal. Proceedings were stalled because two of the accused persons whose cases were slated first did not show up. These were Mr. Solomon Lar and Chief Jim. Nwobodo. The Judge promptly issued a bench warrant for their arrest and detention. The cases were then adjourned till January 16, 1992[59]. This was a convenient means of keeping the politicians out of circulation until after the completion of the gubernatorial and state assembly elections slated for December 14, 1991. Surprisingly, after a joint meeting of the AFRC and the Council of State in Abuja, barely three weeks after the politicians were docked, the government made a *volte face*. It announced that all banned politicians were now unbanned except those who have been convicted in the past and President Babangida, who was banned by the AFRC ostensibly to forestall self-succession[60]. But in September 1992 after the botched presidential primaries twenty three aspirants were banned once again. Ostensibly, this was to sanitise the polity. But it also served the purpose of monitoring and checkmating some influential anti-military elite.

Initially, it appeared as if the government was seriously committed to the transition programme given the flurry of activities within the first few months of the launching of the programme. In fact, by the 3rd and 4th quarters of 1987, performance-enhancing bodies like MAMSER and NEC had started functioning and elections into the Local Government Councils on non-party basis had been successfully conducted. And, by the 2nd quarter of 1988, the Constituent Assembly had been properly constituted while political groups had started emerging. The first serious indication that all was not well with government's handling of the programme was the proscription of the thirteen political associations that were seeking registration with the National Electoral Commission (NEC).

It is worth recalling that NEC had been empowered to employ stringent conditions in the screening of the parties. This was "to eliminate frivolous sectional and undemocratic political associations from the electoral process"[61]. Thus only six of the thirteen associations were deemed to be fairly well put together. It was from these six that the government was expected to pick two as recommended by the Political Bureau. Although the Political Bureau recommended two parties it neither suggested nor mandated the military government to establish the parties[62]. But the government, in its wisdom, decided to proscribe all the political associations and impose two political parties, (the National Republican Convention (NRC) and the Social Democratic Party (SDP)] of its own creation, on the process[63]. This development necessitated the elongation and readjustment of the timetable in order to allow time and space for the imposed parties to gain adherents and commence operations[64].

From the above, it could be seen that the government not only set up the parties but it also took it upon itself to nurture them for sometime "ostensibly to safeguard them from being hijacked by "money bags"[65]. But quite expectedly the 'government parties' never developed a wholesome organic unity and the independent status that they needed to service a democratic arrangement. In fact, members of the parties were mixed grills of strange bedfellows, wayfarers and government stooges. Therefore, they never had close relationship with the masses not to talk of championing their interests. Obviously no result-oriented transition programme could be anchored on this kind of foundation.

On 19 October 1991 primaries were held for governorship aspirants in the states after two major postponements. These were from 24 August and also from 7 September 1991[66]. At the end of the day, 60 winners emerged from the more than 400 aspirants from the two parties. This was the first time that primaries were conducted to nominate governorship candidates[67]. On December 14, State House of Assembly and Governorship elections were held nationwide. The elected governors in the states and their party affiliation are shown below:

TABLE X: List of Elected Governors, 1991 Elections

NO.	STATES	CANDIDATES	PARTY	VOTES
1	Abia	Ogbonnaya Onu	NRC	308,087
2	Adamawa	Sale Michika	NRC	348,586
3	Anambra	Chukwuemeka Ezeife	SDP	261,819
4	Akwa Ibom	Akpan Isemin	NRC	596,840
5	Bauchi	Dahiru Mohammed	NRC	1,435,007
6	Benue	Moses Adamu	SDP	461,039
7	Borno	Maina Ma'aji Lawan	SDP	285,235
8	Cross River	Clement Ebri	NRC	287,519
9	Delta	Felix Ibru	SDP	479,311
10	Edo	John Odigie-Oyegun	SDP	260,442
11	Enugu	Okwesilieze Nwodo	NRC	460,188
12	Imo	Evan Enweren	NRC	386,779
13	Jigawa	Ali Sa'ad Birni-Kudu	SDP	239,410
14	Kaduna	Dabo Lere	NRC	608,550
15	Kano	Kabiru Gaya	NRC	325,145
16	Katsina	Saidu Banda	NRC	290,613
17	Kebbi	Abubakar Musa	NRC	296,961
18	Kogi	Abubakar Audu	NRC	300,319
19	Kwara	Shaaba Lafiagi	SDP	326,739
20	Lagos	Michael Otedola	NRC	424,895
21	Niger	Musa Inuwa	NRC	288,674
22	Ogun	Segun Osoba	SDP	295,402
23	Ondo	Bamidele Olumilua	SDP	374,886
24	Osun	Isiaka Adeleke	SDP	250,638
25	Oyo	Kolapo Ishola	SDP	341,162
26	Plateau	Fidelis Tapgun	SDP	775,101
27	Rivers	Rufus Ada-George	NRC	964,820
28	Sokoto	Yahaya Abdulkarim	NRC	485,889
29	Taraba	Jolly Nyame	SDP	484,090
30	Yobe	Bukar Abba-Ibrahim	SDP	127,935

SDP = 14 NRC = 16

Source: Collated from *Newswatch*, October 28, 1991, p. 9.

With the inauguration of the States' House of Assembly and the swearing-in of the governors in January 1992 a form of diarchy was instituted. The elected legislators and the governors were constrained to relate to and take orders from the ruling military council under the control and direction of General Babangida, the military president.

The next election to be tackled was that of the National Assembly. And as in the previous elections, the politicians were first thrown into disarray before it was eventually conducted on July 4 1992. We can recall that on 26 June 1992, the Secretary to NEC, Aliyu Umar, announced the disqualification of 28 aspirants to the National Assembly for undisclosed reasons other than the so-called security reports. These were 10 Senatorial aspirants and 18 House of Representatives hopefuls[68]. The breakdown on party basis is shown below:

TABLE XI: List of Disqualified Candidates, 1992 National Assembly Elections.

Senatorial Race

NRC (4)	SDP (6)
1. Ibrahim Tahir - Bauchi	1. Umaru Mohammed - Bauchi
2. Umaru Yaro Bida - Borno	2. Sam Mbakwe - Imo
3. C.C. Anyanwu - Imo	3. Wahab Dosumu - Lagos
4. Martin Agbaso - Imo	4. Ebenezer Babatope - Osun
	5. Chris Okolie - Delta
	6. Isa Mohammed - Plateau

House of Representatives

NRC (8)	SDP (10)
1. Yahaya Bunu - Adamawa	1. Isiaku Philmon Tala - Adamawa
2. D.I. Akpagher - Benue	2. Effiok Archibong Uboh – Akwa Ibom
3. Agbo Ella - Benue	3. Mohammed Shamaki - Bauchi
4. William Use Uno - Cross River	4. Bobbo Haruna - Bauchi

5. Mohammed I. Garba - Kaduna	5. Aliyu Adamu - Bauchi
6. Mohammed Hassan Rimi – Kogi	6. Garba Saleh - Bauchi
7.Innocent A. Masi - Rivers	7. K.S.Akom - Cross River
8. Abdullahi S. Illo - Kebbi	8. Kolawole Alawode - Osun
	9. Samuel A. Obafemi - Kogi
	10. James Baitachi - Niger

Source: *Newswatch*, July 13, 1992, p. 9.

On July 4 1992 elections into the National Assembly were conducted nationwide with the Social Democratic Party (SDP) winning majority of the seats in the Senate and the House of Representatives. In the Senate it won 53 seats to the NRC's 38. And in the House of Representatives, the SDP secured 316 seats to the NRC's 277[69]. But the elected legislators were kept in limbo for five months before the National Assembly was inaugurated (on December 5 1992) by President Babangida. It turned out that the newly inaugurated national assembly had been subordinated to the National Defence and Security Council (NDSC) – the replacement for the AFRC – through Decree 53 quietly signed into law three days before its inauguration (i.e. on December 2, 1992)[70].

The National Assembly (Basic Constitutional and Transitional Provisions) Decree 53 of 1992 had limited the legislative competence of the Assembly to non-essential areas. Of the 38 subject areas listed in the 1989 constitution Decree 53 prohibits the Assembly from legislating on 29[71]. Thus the Assembly only maintained a shadowy existence till the termination of the Babangida regime.

Earlier, there had been the blanket banning of the twenty-three presidential aspirants in September 1992. It will be recalled that the presidential primaries in August and September of that year were heavily tainted with corrupt practices, like rigging and outright commercialization of the electoral process with the highest bidders having their ways[72]. Instead of the government to identify the culprits and mete out appropriate punishments

as stipulated in the electoral laws, all the aspirants were banned and the Executive Committees of the two political parties were dissolved at all levels. A new electoral formula known as option A4[73] was devised for another round of primaries.

This development, once again, necessitated adjustments and restructuring of the timetable. The timetable now reads as follows:

30/11/92 – Completion of setting up of caretaker committee at all levels.

23/11/92 - 14/12/92 – Printing of membership cards and registers.

15/12/92 – Distribution of membership cards and registers.

24/12/92 - 3/1/93 – Christmas break.

4/1/93 - 17/1/93 – Call for all prospective aspirants to submit applications to NEC through National Caretaker Committees for screening.

18/1/93 - 31/1/93 – Screening of all aspirants.

6/2/93 – Ward Congress.

20/2/93 – Local Government Congress.

6/3/93 – State Congress.

7/3/93 - 26/3/93 – State flag bearers Campaign for National Convention.

27/3/93 - 29/3/93 – National Convention (NRC, SDP).

30/3/93 - 11/4/93 – Caretaker Committees handover.

15/4/93 - 18/4/93 – Elected Executives prepare for Campaigns.

19/4/93 - 11/6/93 – Electioneering Campaigns.

12/6/93 – Election.

13/6/93 - 20/6/93 – Declaration of results.

21/6/93 - 26/8/93 – Setting up of Election Tribunal, sitting and judgements.

27/8/93 – Swearing-in[74].

The new electoral formula (option A4) eventually produced the party flag-bearers. These were Alhaji Ibrahim Tofa of the NRC and Chief M.K.O. Abiola of the SDP. The presidential election slated for June 12 1993 was held against all odds. For instance, on the 10th June 1993, at an unusual time of 9.15p.m., an Abuja High Court (at the instance of an illegal pro-military body-Association for Better Nigerians (ABN)][75] restrained NEC from conducting the election. But NEC ignored the injunction claiming immunity under Decree 13 of 1993 which had ousted the jurisdiction of any law court over matters pertaining to the conduct of the presidential election. The election was widely acclaimed as free, fair and credible and was believed to have been won by Chief Abiola of the SDP. The table below attests to this:

TABLE XII: States' Presidential Elections Results, 1993

S/NO	STATE	SDP SCORE	SDP %	NRC SCORE	NRC %	TOTAL SCORE
1.	Abia	105,273	41.04	151,227	58.96	256,500
2.	Adamawa	140,875	45.72	167,239	54.28	308,114
3.	Akwa Ibom	224,787	51.86	199,342	48.14	414,129
4.	Anambra	212,024	57.11	159,258	42.89	371,282
5.	Bauchi	339,339	39.27	524,836	60.73	864,175
6.	Benue	246,830	56.94	186,302	43.06	433,132
7.	Borno	153,496	54.40	128,684	45.60	282,180
8.	Cross River	189,303	55.23	153,452	44.77	342,278
9	Delta	327,277	69.30	154,001	30.70	308,979
10.	Edo	205,407	66.48	103,572	33.52	308,979
11.	Enugu	263,101	48.09	284,050	51.91	547,151
12.	Imo	159,350	44.86	195,836	55.14	355,186
13.	Jigawa	138,552	60.67	89,836	38.33	228,388
14.	Kaduna	389,713	52.20	356,860	47.80	746,573
15.	Kano	169,619	52.28	154,809	47.72	324,428
16.	Katsina	171,162	38.70	271,077	61.30	442,239
17	Kebbi	70,219	32.66	144,808	67.34	215,492
18	Kogi	222,760	45.60	265,732	54.40	488,492
19	Kwara	272,270	77.24	80,209	22.78	352,479
20	Lagos	883,965	85.54	149,432	14.46	1,033,397
21	Niger	136,350	38.10	221,437	61.90	357,787
22	Ogun	425,725	87.78	59,246	12.22	484,971

23	Ondo	883,024	84.42	162,994	15.58	1,046,018
24	Osun	365,266	83.52	72,068	16.48	437,334
25	Oyo	536,266	83.52	105,788	16.48	641,799
26	Plateau	417,565	61.68	259,394	38.32	676,959
27	Rivers	370,678	36.63	640,973	63.37	1,011,551
28	Sokoto	97,726	20.79	372,250	79.21	469,976
29	Taraba	101,887	61.42	64,001	38.58	165,888
30	Yobe	111,887	63.59	664,061	38.41	775,948
31	FCT Abuja	19,968	52.16	18,313	47.84	38,281
	TOTAL	8,341,309	58.36	6,952,087	41.64	14,293,396

Source: *The News*, 28 June 1993, P. 24.

Ordinarily what remained to be done was for NEC to officially announce the winner and bring the transition to a close. But NEC announced the results midway before abandoning its responsibilities thereby keeping the whole nation in suspense. Three days after the period designated for the announcement of results had elapsed, precisely on the 23rd of June, the government pronounced an annulment of the election on the grounds that it wanted to "protect the nation's legal system and judiciary from being ridiculed and politicized nationally and internationally"[76].

Obviously this was a nebulous excuse as the judiciary was not experiencing any difficulty that could not be redressed without scuttling the transition programme. Granted that the courts had been inundated with cases before and after the June 12 polls, it must be remembered that this was warranted by the anti-democratic stand of some pro-military bodies that were bent on disrupting the transition programme, as we have observed previously. Howbeit, the courts were coping well and it was when the various court judgements were taking some definitive shapes that would have put the government in a quandary that it moved to do the "rescue mission". Not only this, government also ordered the suspension of NEC and the abrogation of Decree 52 of 1992 and Decree 13 of 1993 which gave legal backing to the transition programme. It proceeded further to announce a new transition timetable with another round of election slated for 31st July 1993.

The newly reconstituted NEC released a revised timetable which read thus:

July 1993

2nd - Talks between NEC, Government and Political Parties.

3rd - 6th – Political parties, NEC to devise means of nomination of candidates including conventions.

7th - 10th – Nomination of candidates by political parties.

10th – 30th – Campaigns of political parties.

31st – Election.

August 1993

3rd – Results

4th - 10th – Election petitions in the Supreme Court.

11th -25th – Briefing of President-elect.

27th – Swearing-in of the new president[77].

This time around, the 'transition weary' civil populace saw through the charade that the transition had become and so they snubbed this new arrangement. Calls for the respect for peoples' choice as expressed in the June 12 poll started reverbrating across the country.

This made the IBB regime to be very much uncomfortable in office. It therefore started working towards a dignified exit that would still leave the military as the preponderant force. The regime eventually manoeuvred the compromising political class into accepting and conferring credibility on an Interim National Government (ING), headed by Chief Ernest Shonekan, to which it reluctantly handed over on the 26th of August, 1993. This unconstitutional arrangement barely lasted for three months before it was terminated through coup which brought the military back to power once again.

Prominent members of the political class (among whom was Chief M.K.O. Abiola, who was recently robbed of his electoral victory) were said to have goaded the military into carrying out the coup. According to General Sani Abacha[78], the new Head of

State, "Chief Abiola not only publicly called upon the military to intervene, he actively participated in selecting the broad-based cabinet of the new administration"[79].

IBB also blamed Abacha's overthrow of the ING on "the public, the society, the politicians (who) were not prepared to give the interim government a chance"[80]. But we must remember that the ING was unconstitutional as it was never part of the transition agenda *ab initio*. It was only smuggled-in to create a leeway for the discredited military[81]. It is to be expected, there-fore, that it would not be popular with the populace. Thus, the call, by some Nigerians to the military to rescue them from the ING, naïve as it may seem, was expected to be a short term expe-diency before the issue of annulment of the June 12 election is revisited. It is within this context that we can view Abiola's initial warm embrace and cooperative relationship with the Abacha regime. But Gen. Abacha capitalized on Abiola's initial stand on his regime to paint him (Abiola) as a colluding elite and a pillar of support for the regime.

The new regime referred to itself as a 'child of necessity' and promised to relinquish power as soon as the lingering political log-jam (which the events post-dating the June 12 polls brought to life) is straightened[82]. But based on the now familiar history of military involvement in politics in Nigeria, this turned out to be yet another ruse. Indications to this end started showing by January 1994 when the new regime launched what it called 'The New Direction'[83]. Obviously, this was precursory to the drafting of another long-drawn transition programme.From the foregoing discussions, some general observations on the nature and orienta-tion of the transition programme under the military are consid-ered necessary. The section below will be devoted to this task.

GENERAL OBSERVATIONS ON TRANSITION PROGRAMMES UNDER MILITARY TUTELAGE

What we have done in the preceding sections is an examina-tion of the individual regime's transition programme, highlight-ing in the process their peculiarities and end results. However,

there were some similar traits in the programming and implementation of the transition which, when viewed critically, leads one to the conclusion that the transition programme was a military strategy for survival and perpetuation in office. This is so because fundamentally, it portrayed civilians as political neophytes or sophomores who needed to be put through the rubrics of politics and governance before they could be entrusted with political power. The position of the military was that until the politicians have learned their lessons the people would have to continue to put up with military rule.

Since the January 1966 coup, the impression had been created that the military was a neutral and superior organization that could be relied upon to stabilize or radicalize the system. Thus, the fact that the same military had been initiating the transition agenda gave the impression that it was genuinely interested in radical political transformation. But we were constantly made to believe that the change had not taken place because the civil populace was ill-prepared. This was the rational basis for the perennial transition exercises which really prolonged military rule instead of ensuring quick disengagement.

For instance, the disengagement that took place in October 1979 and also that of August 1993 did not lead to the enthronement of democracy not so much because the civil populace was not properly prepared as of the fact of the deliberate manipulation of the process by the military and its civilian stooges. It is therefore not surprising that the disengagement only served as a short term expediency during which the 'incompetence' of the civil political class was exposed to the generality of the people. This then prepared the ground for the return of the 'corrective' military in a more formidable manner. In other words, as a result of the vested interests of the military sponsors of the transition programme and the self-seeking orientation of their civilian collaborators, the political environment was always crisis-laden. The military then waited in the wings watching out for the usual promptings from the disillusioned segments of the society before staging a 'reluctant' comeback. This situation has been

aptly described by Olufemi Akinola as the "handback option"[84]. Therefore we are inclined to perceive the disengagement/transition agenda as a ruse.

As further reinforcement of the view expressed above, it is important to note that all the transition programmes ever embarked upon by the military in Nigeria were imposed on the polity. The familiar trend was for a new junta to announce a transition programme and proceed by issuing decrees, organizing consultative assembly, constitutional council, review or commission, and dictating the rules of the game at every stage. Even in the case of the IBB regime in which a Political Bureau was set up to ascertain the wishes of the people, the government still imposed its views on the people.

Furthermore, rhetorical pronouncements and real actions were always at variance in the implementation of the transition programmes. While on paper the programmes always appeared to be well-thought out and patriotically motivated, they were usually manipulated towards a pre-conceived end which always left the military as the preponderant political force. This is to be expected because the fact that the military was the group initiating, packaging and implementing the transition programmes gave it profound political clout. Thus, it dictated the pace, timing and quality of political activities. This puts it in a favourable position to determine the outcome of the programme. Even the 1979 exercise which appears to negate the above observation eventually turned out to the advantage of the military as we have shown.

The Babangida transition exercise stood out from others before it as the acme of manipulation and devious manoeuvres. As far back as 1989, Leo Dare had observed that the Babangida regime was "fast acquiring a reputation for its policy of deliberate destabilization of political actors"[85]. The major indices of this development were the frequent use of banning, disqualification, arrests, the constant movement of key officers around and the dissolution and reconstitution of the AFRC and NEC. This policy orientation created instability and a dependency on the president. The uncertainty which the implementation of the policy

engendered induced in subordinates and some aspiring politicians uncritical obedience in order to please the boss and secure their tenure or actualize their aspirations as the case may be[86]. This situation was quite open to manipulations and intrigues.

The most striking example of manipulated transition was the ING arrangement to which the IBB regime reluctantly handed over in August 1993. It is interesting to note that the number two man in the ING (Gen. Sani Abacha) was the only Service Chief that was not retired before the IBB regime handed over. His (Abacha's) placement in the ING partly explains the ease with which he toppled the civilian-led government on the 17th of November 1993. In fact, it has been alleged in some quarters that IBB deliberately left Gen. Abacha behind in order to pave way for the protection of the interest of the military and the actualization of the latter's ambition[87]. But, in a recent press interview, IBB defended his action by saying that Abacha was left behind because he was holding a political appointment[88]. However, it must be remembered that Abacha's so-called political appointment was within the context of a ' military government and so in order to ensure a kind of continuity he was retained to serve in the ING. This fits into our submission that the military never contemplated total withdrawal from the political arena.

Howbeit, one incontrovertible fact that has emerged so far is that the recurring nature of coups and countercoups in Nigeria did not only militarise the political environment, it also caused political atrophy, apathy and cynicism, which resulted in the subordination of the civil populace and the political ascendancy of the military[89]. Thus, there existed for sometime in Nigeria a political climate unwittingly supportive of continued military usurpation of political power. It was the unmasking of General Babangida that served as the eye-opener.

Therefore, the Nigerian experience during the period studied shows that the military class did not sincerely execute any programme that would have eroded its power and influence on a permanent basis. The romance with transition programmes (which kept the civil populace busy) was a diversionary tactics

which gave the military regimes the much needed credibility and breathing space. This assisted in prolonging the life of some regimes as we have noted.

Notes

1. The programme was originally billed to end in 1976, but it was abandoned in 1974.
2. For details, see, A.H.M. Kirk-Greene: *Crisis and Conflict in Nigeria: A Documentary Source Book,* Vol. 1 (London: O.U.P., 1971) pp. 158-159.
3. A. Kirk-Greene and D. Rimmer: *Nigeria Since 1970: A Political and Economic Outline* (London: Hodder and Stoughton, 1981) p.4.
4. West Africa, 26 December 1970 1ˢᵗ January 1971, p. 1502.
5. Ibid.
6. L.O. Dare: *The Praetorian Trap: The Problems and Prospects of Military Disengagement* – Inaugural Lecture, Obafemi Awolowo University, Ile-Ife, 1989. p. 19.
7. See, B. Dudley: *An Introduction to Nigerian Government and Politics* (London: Macmillan Publishers Ltd., 1982) pp. 116-120.
8. See, J.O. Ojiako: *13 Years of Military Rule* (Lagos: Daily Times Publication, 1979) p. 77.
9. Ibid. pp. 77-78.
10. See, Dare: *The Praetorian Trap...* p. 19.
11. Ibid.
12. Ibid. p. 20.
13. O. Obasanjo: *Not My Will* (Ibadan: Ibadan University Press, 1990) pp. 49-50.
14. See, NAI/SD/MS – *Mohammed His Excellency, Brigadier M.R.;* : Head of the Federal Military Government, Commander in Chief of the Armed Forces of the Federal Republic of Nigeria: A Programme for Political Action, 1ˢᵗ October, 1975.
15. Dare: p. 20.
16. One of the nominated members, Chief Obafemi Awolowo, declined to serve. Only 49 members carried out the task.
17. See, Ojiako: 13 Years ... pp. 103-104.
18. Ibid. p. 106.

19. Gen. M. Mohammed had been killed in an abortive coup on 13th February 1976. Significantly, this unsettling development did not derail the transition programme.

20. See, NAI/NC/A7 – Proceeding of the Constituent Assembly Official Report, nos. 1-9, 1978 vols. I and II.

21. See, NAI/NC/A9 – The Constitution of the Federal Republic of Nigeria 1979.

22. See, NAI/SD/025 – *Obasanjo, Segun:* Towards Civil Rule – Speeches on Preparations for changing over to civilian government in 1979.

23. Ibid..

24. Ojiako: p.195.

25. Ibid. p.193.

26. Ibid.

27. Ibid, pp. 202-203.

28. Ibid, pp. 204-206.

29. Ibid. p.207.

30. NAI/PX/G7F – The General Elections, 1979: Report by Federal Electoral Commission, p.5

31. Ibid.

32. Ibid. p. 6.

33. Ibid.

34. See, *Electoral Decree no 73 of 1977 (section 34A(2) and Electoral Amendment Decree 32 of 1978 (Section 34A(3)}.*

35. See, James Oluleye: *Military Leadership in Nigeria, 1966-1979* (Ibadan: I.U.P., 1985) p. 206.

36. Ibid.

37. E. Babatope: *Not His Will: The Awolowo – Obasanjo Wager,*(Benin City: Jodah Publications, 1990). p. 9.

38. Ibid. p. 10.

39. L.O. Dare: The Praetorian Trap... p. 21.

40. See, Toyin Falola and Julius Ihonvbere: *The Rise and Fall of Nigeria's Second Republic, 1979-1984* (London: Zed Book Ltd., 1985); and, Richard Joseph: *Democracy and Prebendal Politics in Nigeria: The Rise and Fall of the Second Republic* (Ibadan: Spectrum Books Ltd., 1991).

41. See, Introduction.

42. L.O. Dare: p. 23.

43. See, O. Olagunju and S.E. Oyovbaire: *For Their Tomorrow We Gave Our Today: Selected Speeches of IBB, Vol. II* (Ibadan: Safari Books Ltd., 1991) p. 107.

44. The Objectives of SAP and the Strategies for achieving them are contained in the budget speech of 1986. See, O. Olagunju: *Portrait of a New Nigeria: Selected Speeches of IBB, Vol. 1* (Lagos: Precision Press, n.d.) pp. 131-162.

45. For penetrating insights into the effect of SAP on IBB's 'Democratisation process, see, S.O. J. Ojo: "Regulating the Polity in a Deregulated Economy: Hypothesis and Illustrations Based on the Structural Adjustment Programme and Transition to Civil Rule Programme", in S. G. Tyoden (ed.): *Transition to Civil Rule Programme; The Journey So Far* (Lagos: NPSA, 1992) pp. 8-26; See also Ibrahim, F.O: "IBB's Year of Destiny", in *Daily Times*, 1st January 1993, p. 11.

46. See, *Government Views and Comments on the Findings and Recommendations of the Political Bureau* (Abuja: MAMSER, 1987) pp. 1-2.

47. Ibid, p. 16; See also, *Political Bureau Report* (Abuja: MAMSER, 1987).

48. Speech delivered by General Ibrahim Babangida on the occasion of the 10th Graduation Ceremony of the National Institute of Policy and Strategic Studies (NIPSS) Kuru, 31 October, 1987, p. 15.

49. See, Government's Views ..., p. 88.

50. Larry Diamond: "Nigeria's Search For a New Political Order", in *Journal of Democracy* 2(2) Spring 1991, p. 54.

51. See, Olagunju and Oyovbaire: Portrait Of a New Nigeria... p. 94.

52. According to a newspaper report the programme was tinkered with 39 times; see, *Sunday Tribune*, 4 July 1993; p. 12.

53. See, *Newswatch*, December 30, 1991, p. 26

54. Ibid.

55. Ibid.

56. Ibid.

57. See, *Newswatch*, December 16, 1991. pp. 33-34.

58. Ibid. pp. 32.

59. Ibid. p. 35.

60. See, *Newswatch*, December 30, 1991, p. 25.

61. See, S. Oyovbaire and O. Olagunju (eds.): *Foundations of a New Nigeria: The IBB Era* (London: Precision Press, 1989) p. 31.

62. See, *Report of the Political Bureau* (Abuja: MAMSER, 1989). p. 131.

63. See, *Transition to Civil Rule (Political Parties Registration and Activities) Decree 27 of 1989*, (Abuja MAMSER, 1989) and *Newswatch*, 23 October, 1989, pp. 13-17.

64. See, *Transition Programme (Amendment) Decree 26, 1989* reproduced from Federal Republic of Nigeria Official Gazette No. 69, 17th December 1989, Vol. 76, pp. 32-33.

65. Ajayi: Babangida's Transition Programme... p. 75.

66. See, *African Concord*, 21 October 1991. p. 42.

67. See, *Newswatch*, 28 October 1991. p. 9.

68. See, *Newswatch*, 13 July, 1992. p. 9.

69. See, *Newswatch*, July 20, 1992. p. 17

70. See, *The African Guardian*, December 21, 1992. p. 15.

71. Ibid.

72. For details, see the following *African Concord*, 7 September 1992, p. 50 and *African Concord*, 5 October 1992, pp. 22-24.

73. See, NEC: *The ABC of Option A4* (Abuja: NEC, 1992).

74. Ibid. p. 13.

75. For details of the nefarious activities of ABN and other pro-military groups (like Third eye and League of patriots) See, *The African Guardian, 28th* December, 1992 pp. 18-21: Ibid., 21st June 1993, pp. 11-13; *This Week* 3rd May 1993, pp. 8-15; and, Dada P.A. and Alao, A :"The ABN's Pandora Box", in Sunday Tribune, 25 July 1993, pp. 8 & 9.

76. See, *Daily Times*, 24 June 1993 pp. 1 & 20.

77. See, *Sunday Tribune*, 4 July 1993, p. 1

78. General Sani Abacha was the Chief of Defence Staff under IBB and the second-in-command in the ING contraption headed by Chief Ernest Shonekan. So the putsch which brought him to power was more like a palace coup.

79. See, Federal Republic of Nigeria, 35th Independence Anniversary Address by Gen. Sani Abacha, GCON, dss, mni, Head of State and Commander-in-Chief of the Armed Forces of the Federal Republic of Nigeria, on 1st October, 1995, (Abuja: National Ori-

entation Agency, 1995) p. 11; see also, *The News*, 13 December 1993 pp. 19 & 24.

80. See, *Tell*, 7 December 1998, p. 18.

81. Gani Fawehinmi: *June 12 Crisis: The Illegality of Shonekan's Government* (Lagos: Nigerian Law Publications, 1993).

82. See, *The News*, 29 November, 1993, Cover Story – "Abacha's Agenda".

83. National Orientation Agency (NOA): *The New Direction* (Abuja: NOA, 1994)

84. Olufemi Akinola: "The Authoritarian Creation of Political Order: Military Rule, The Handback Option and Democratisation in Nigeria," in *Proceedings of the 16th Annual Conference of the Nigerian Political Science Association (NPSA)*, Calabar 1989.

85. Dare: The Praetorian trap... p. 24.

86. Ibid.

87. For details, of the alleged 'IBB-Abacha Pact' see, the exclusive interview with Professor Omo Omoruyi (former Director-General of the Centre for Democratic Studies) in *Tell*, 29 September 1997, pp. 20-22.

88. *Tell*, 7 December 1998, p. 18

89. See, Akin Akindele: *The Military Eranchise* (Chapel Hill: Professional Press, 1993) p. 96.

CHAPTER SIX

CONCLUSION:
THE VIRTUAL COLLAPSE OF
THE NIGERIAN STATE

For the period covered by this study (1966-1993), the military evolved and perfected some survival strategies which enabled it to monopolise political power in Nigeria. These strategies have been highlighted and discussed in the preceding chapters and the following conclusions can be drawn.

First, the 'corrective regime' posturing not only assisted in securing legitimacy for military juntas, it also portrayed members of the civil political class as inept and irresponsible. Therefore, they were not to be entrusted with political power. This contributed immeasurably to the political ascendancy and dominance of the military.

Second, the careful employment of patronage and cooptation by different military regimes compromised the political class and also polarized the civil society. This is reminiscent of the divide and rule tactics of the colonial administration. The end result was a weakened civil society that was unable to put up concerted resistance against the military for a long time.

Third, the deliberate employment of coercive and repressive methods cowed down the citizenry, and the political class was subordinated through intimidation. This development engendered political apathy and nonchalance. Wittingly or unwittingly, this kind of situation encouraged prolonged military usurpation of power. But the militarized political environment caused political atrophy and low level of socio-economic development, which eventually alienated the people from military rule.

Fourth, the regular initiation of transition programmes, ostensibly to facilitate military disengagement, served sinister motives. The 'hidden agenda', in nearly all the cases dealt with was the perpetuation of military rule through cunning devices. The political class and the civil society were usually held responsible for the 'failed' transition programmes. Therefore, they had to put up with military regimes until such a time that they would have learnt their lessons. Thus, instead of facilitating military disengagement from politics, the transition programmes actually prolonged its hold on political power.

However, the long stay of the military in the corridors of power and the employment of the aforementioned strategies for political control had deleterious impact on the military establishment and the polity. By the time of the Babangida regime (especially towards its end) the cleavages in the society and the military had become so pronounced that the existence of the nation as a corporate entity was seriously threatened. We can recall that as early as 1989, L.O. Dare had drawn attention to the destabilizing effect of political adventurism on the military. He observed that "political involvement accentuates the cleavages among the armed forces. The frequency of coups against military regimes bring into clear relief the nature of these divisions"[1]. He went ahead to identify the nature of the divisions as "ethnic, class, generational cleavages or may be divisions among those who have tasted political office and those who have not, who may now like their own opportunity. These make coups endemic"[2].

The situation was compounded by Babangida's opportunistic management of the military in order to secure its loyalty through subordination. He employed a two-pronged strategy which can be summarized as follows: (i) He was constantly relieving senior officers of important military command posts, retiring them and compensating them with lucrative political offices. (ii) Up-and-coming younger officers are thereby given the opportunity to move up and occupy the posts vacated by the senior officers[3]. This strategy enabled the Babangida regime to contain some 'radical' middle level officers. But many more officers could not be pla-

cated in this manner because; first, the appointments could not go round because of the large number of people to be taken care of[4], and second, there was also the fact of the doubtful loyalty of some of them. This development further polarized the armed forces pitching the beneficiaries of government patronage against those left out. This class of officers (i.e. those left out) could as well be bidding their time to stage their own coup. Adekanye has rightly asserted that "the 17 November 1993 coup that toppled Babangida's interim government must be seen in this light"[5].

Thus, by the time Babangida was vacating office the military had been 'visibly' polarised into two major factions – the Babangida loyalists or "Babangida Boys" (in local parlance) and the others. His corrosive machiavellian tactics was largely responsible for this development. The situation was further compounded by his political misadventure which reached its high point with the annulment of the June 12 presidential election for no just cause. His regime bequeathed to the nation a badly ruptured and discredited military organization; and, a disillusioned, politically disoriented and weakened polity. In fact the nation was brought to the brink of disintegration with voices of secession and restructuring becoming louder by the day[6]. While the Southern elements were insisting on the actualization of the June 12 election results or going their separate ways, the northern elements were apathetic.

It was the coming to power of Gen. Sani Abacha, unpleasant as it was, that saved the country from disintegration. This happened in two ways: First, Abacha came to power on the platform of a 'reactive intervener' professing to right things[7]. In this way he was able to coopt some influential people (especially some members of the aggrieved SDP like, Alhaji Lateef Jakande; Chief Ebenezer Babatope; Mr. Solomon Lar and Alhaji Baba Gana Kingibe, the Vice President designate) into his government. This ensured the support of a cross section of people and so the regime was able to buy time to consolidate before showing its true colour. Second, after settling down in office Abacha forcefully held the country together in an authoritarian fashion through

coercion and repression on an unprecedented scale. The idea of a Sovereign National Conference to debate the future of the country was severely frowned at and the peddlers of such ideas – the pro-democracy, human rights organizations, the Press and some radical unions – were constantly harassed and threatened with annihilation.

It was in this 'Stalinist' way that Nigeria was held together from November 17 1993 until the termination of the Abacha regime about five years thereafter. Since this period is outside the scope of our study we will not comment more on it. Our main concern for now is to establish the fact that the generality of the people had become tired of military rule and its noxious impact on the nation. In fact, the articulate segments of the civil society had been offering alternatives to military regime before now. The Abacha experience only served to further reinforce the peoples' resolve. Some of the suggestions offered include the formalisation of diarchy; popular uprising against military rulers; establishment of a Coup Prevention Council, extending basic military training to members of the NYSC initially and later to all undergraduates in Nigerian tertiary institutions; liberalising gun laws; having regional armies and passive resistance to military political power usurpers until they are forced to relinquish power. We will proceed to appraise these options in the order in which they are listed above.

As far back as 1974, Dr. Nnamdi Azikiwe, Nigeria's first Head of State, had advocated for a political alliance between the military and the civilians in the governance of the country[8]. Also in 1984, Arthur Nwankwo, apparently piqued by the recurrent nature of military rule in Nigeria, recommended a political arrangement that would incorporate civilians, the military and democracy[9]. The informing sensibility was that given the preponderant nature of the military in Nigeria's political landscape and the fact that civilians have been servicing military regimes, a political arrangement that would formalize civilian imputs into military administrations should be evolved[10]. In other words, the responsibility for running the state should be shared between the civilians and military men.

It is our belief that the diarchy option is not feasible in Nigeria for the following reasons. First, the rigid and authoritarian disposition of the military cannot be easily made amenable to democratic orientation. Second, the election or selection process would be crisis-laden given the 'winner-takes-all' political orientation in Nigeria. Third, even if such a government is eventually constituted there would be a high degree of overlaps, uncoordinated functions and frictions resulting from the attempt on the part of either of the constituent partners to exert influence on the polity. In practical terms, this kind of arrangement would only serve as a short term expediency before a full-blown military rule is reinstated. The example of the Interim National Government (ING) set up by the IBB regime in August 1993 readily comes to mind here. The ING, which was a facsimile of the proposition discussed above, lasted for barely three months before it was toppled by General Abacha (the erstwhile second-in-command under the ING).

The observation above must have forcibly struck the pro-democracy, human rights and other radical groups in Nigeria when they advocated popular uprising as the means towards dislodging the military from power. But the anti-military campaign was not coordinated until 1993. Before 1993 the resistance against military rule was carried on in a piecemeal fashion by different pro-democracy and human rights' groups. But this changed when the Campaign for Democracy (CD), an umbrella organization for many radical groups[11], spearheaded a 'military must go' campaign which opened with popular uprising in July 1993. But this was a risky (almost foolhardy) move given the brutal and repressive disposition of the military to the civil society. In fact it cost many people their lives and freedom[12].

Moreover, we can recall that while it is true that popular uprising assisted in the demise of the IBB regime, the military still 'elbowed' its way to power within a few months and remained in office till 29th May 1999. The point must be emphasized that the military had become so entrenched in power and enjoyed the active support of some important segments and influential

personalities[13] in the polity that it required a yeoman's effort to displace it in 1999.This feat was achieved through the combination of internal and external pressures.

In 1988 members of the Constituent Assembly had suggested the establishment of a Coup Prevention Council to mobilize Nigerians to reject any government that comes to power through undemocratic means[14]. This was not altogether new as Section 1(2) of the 1979 Constitution had invalidated coups. Yet many coups did happen thereafter. It must be stated that coup plotters do not require the mandate of the constitution or any governmental agency before carrying out their deeds. And just as the case was for past constitutions, any so-called coup prevention council would be one of the first casualties of a successful coup[15].

It has been established that the military found it relatively easy to seize control of power because of its monopoly of weapons of violence. And that if that monopoly were to be broken, it will be difficult to execute coups. This led Dare to suggest that basic military training be given to members of the National Youth Service Corps (NYSC) and undergraduates in the tertiary institutions. This crop of people would constitute a form of counter force against military political adventurism[16]. In addition it has also been suggested that those civilian beneficiaries of military training should be allowed to possess weapons both for self-protection and for launching counter offensive against coups[17]. The snag here is that these can only be relied upon as long-term strategies.

Also an option that has gained currency in recent time (especially in the Southern part of the country) is the idea of breaking the monolithic character of the military by having regional armies. It is believed that under this kind of arrangement it would be difficult for the military to muster enough support to take over government at the center. But the problem here is that this option can only be feasible under a confederal system. What this amounts to is that before such an option can be practicalised in Nigeria, there would have to be fundamental restructuring of the polity to reflect the kind of looseness implicit in the option.

Definitely the military would not want to embrace this option. Even civilians would have to agree in a Sovereign National Conference or the National Assembly (as the case may be) before such moves can be initiated by the civilian government. In our reckoning, a good starting point for safeguarding the Nigerian State from military political adventurism would be the adoption of passive resistance to, and mass boycott of, military impostors by civilians. It is gratifying to note that many influential Nigerians are now coming to this realization. For instance, Chief Gani Fawehinmi, the renowned social crusader, has been advocating in recent times, what he calls 'Ghandism', that is, civil disobedience, as a means of resisting military rule in future[18]. Also Nigeria's former military ruler and current civilian President, Chief Olusegun Obasanjo recently came out forcefully in support of this option. In a thanksgiving speech after his release from prison in June 1998 he said,

> Nigerians must resolve that any future military adventurism into our political life must be met with stiff non-violent resistance and total withdrawal of service-public and private- complete non-participation, non-fraternisation and non-cooperation. Stiff punishment must be prescribed for those who covertly break this national ethos[19].

It is important to note that the history of Nigeria under the military has shown that the military could not successfully impose itself on the nation without the support of civilians either as props, technocrats, advisers or 'image- launderers'. If this often exploited support is denied, the military would be handicapped and so compelled to concentrate on its constitutional role of safeguarding the security and territorial integrity of the nation. One way of achieving this objective is to have an All Politicians' meeting where they must resolve to resist military overlordship and prescribe sanctions for erring members.

We recognize the danger posed to this option by the deeply entrenched network of patronages, ethnic loyalties and the attraction of public offices for the purpose of private accumula-

tion. But we still believe that this is a less hazardous and more promising option if we can appeal successfully to the patriotic instincts of, or prevail on, the colluding elites to conform. Thereafter, there would be a need for the civilian government again to initiate some moves that would discourage military usurpation of power in future. First, the civilians should have learnt some useful lessons from past experiences by conducting themselves and the affairs of state in such a way that they will not provide the military with an excuse to take over the government. IBB once remarked in a press interview that "(We) in the military are very smart people we wouldn't interfere in government when we know it has the support of the populace"[20].

It must be strongly emphasized that the only antidote to military takeover of government is good governance based on justice and fairplay. In order to make assurance double sure, people should also be sensitized to the evil impact of military regime through the establishment of a Truth and Justice Commission to look into the activities of the military in government. The civil society must also be encouraged to change its placid attitude through the organization and sustenance of civil defence resistance movements against military usurpation of power.

Second, the civilian government should take the following practical steps to keep the military in check.

(i) The numerical strength of the military must be reduced to a manageable proportion and its personnel must be well trained and kitted to enhance professionalism;

(ii) Borrowing from the experience of the developed countries (like Britain and the United States of America) and even less developed ones (like India and Israel) the military must be constantly engaged in border patrols, road constructions, rescue missions and general preparation for an 'imminent war' in order to keep it gainfully employed;

(iii) a carefully packaged re-orientation programme (or 'debriefing') must be put in place to refocus the attention of the military towards its primary objective, that is, safeguarding the territorial integrity of the nation;

(iv) a comprehensive welfare programme that would render political adventurism less attractive must be articulated and implemented without unnecessary delay.

(v) All military officers who have held political appointments of whatever nature should be retired. Only recently some military officers in this category were retired by the civilian administration of Chief Olusegun Obasanjo. But there are some officers still in the service who presumably held minor political appointments. Such officers should also be retired.

Third, the support of international organizations like the United Nations Organisation, the Commonwealth of Nations, African Union and the Economic Community of West African States must be enlisted to keep the military at bay. The recent experience in Sierra Leone where ECOMOG forces were used to dislodge the military usurpers from power and reinstate the democratic regime of Ahmed Tejan Kabbah[21] is indicative of the viability of this strategy.

It has also been suggested by a politician[22] that the civilian government should sign a pact with the United States of America for the defence and sustenance of democracy. The danger here lies in the fact that once the Americans manage to entrench themselves in the country it will be very difficult to get them out eventually. But the suggestion indicated the strong desire to keep the military out of politics.

In short, all conceivable and realistic efforts must be made to shore-up the civilian government that has managed to wrest political power from the military since 1999. This is informed by the belief that the worst civilian regime still has a better potential of initiating or facilitating genuine democratic governance. The long stay of the military in the corridors of power and its mismanagement of the nation's politics and economy over the years have exposed the lie in its 'corrective regime' posturing. This observation is not hidden from the domestic and international communities. They only need to be properly sensitized

and mobilized to assist in resisting the military political power usurpers if and when they rear their heads again.

The fact that civilians had been in power since May 29, 1999 should not be interpreted to mean that the military has been silenced permanently.We can recall that in April 2004 shortly after the controversial local government elections a coup attempt or what the civilian government, in its own wisdom, called breach of security was nipped in the bud[23].This unsettling development is a sure pointer to the fact that military men have not given up totally the desire to seize power given the right opportunity.Controversial elections have been known to provide such opportunities in the past[24].

Thus, the incumbent civilian administration should endeavour to conduct free and fair elections and improve markedly on its social welfare programmes if the present democratic experiment is to endure.

Notes

1. L.O. Dare: *The Praetorian Trap: The Problems and Prospects of Military Disengagement* – Inaugural Lecture, O.A.U., Ile-Ife, 1989, p. 26.

2. Ibid.

3. See, J. 'Bayo Adekanye: "The Military in the Transition", in Larry Diamond, et al: *Transition Without End: Nigerian Politics and Civil Society Under Babangida,* (Ibadan: Vantage Publishers, 1997) p. 72.

4. Ibid. p. 76

5. Ibid.

6. See, *The Guardian*, 6 September 1993. pp. 9, 15 & 16; *Newswatch*, 30 August, 1993, pp. 26-27; and *Nigerian Tribune*, 6 July 1993, p. 1.

7. See, A.A. Agagu: "The Abacha Regime and Political Order in Nigeria", in Dipo Kolawole and N.O. Mimiko (eds.): *Political Democratisation and Economic Deregulation in Nigeria under the Abacha Administration, 1993-1998* (Ado Ekiti: OSUA, 1998) pp. 41-48.

8. See, N. Azikiwe: *Democracy with Military Vigilance* (Nzukka: Africa Book Company, 1974).

9. Arthur Nwankwo: *Civilianised Soldiers: Army – Civilian Government for Nigeria* (Enugu: Fourth Dimension Pub. Coy Ltd., 1984) pp. xi-xii.

10. Ibid. p. 17

11. See, Tunde Babawale: "Crisis, Adjustment and Popular Empowerment", in CDHR: *Nigeria: Non-Governmental Organisations and Democracy* (Lagos: Friedrich Ebert Foundation, 1997) p. 20.

12. See, the following: CDHR: Annual Report (1993); CLO: *Annual Report on Human Rights in Nigeria* (1993) and *Victims* – CDHR newsletter (several editions).

13. See, above, Chapter Three; See also, Braimah Idaye: "The Abiola Issue" in *Sunday Concord*, 24 March 1996, p.9.

14. See, *The Guardian* 30 January, 1989.

15. See, Dare: pp. 26-27.

16. Ibid. p. 27.

17. Ibid.

18. See, *Nigerian Tribune*, 22 April 1998, p. 18.

19. See, *Nigerian Tribune*, 22 June 1998, p. 24 and *Tell*, 6 July 1998, p. 33.

20. *Tell*, 7 December 1998, p. 25,

21. For details, see *Africa Today*, April 1998, pp. 12-14

22. Personality Interview with Dr. R.O. Mimiko, Ondo State Commissioner for Health and Social Welfare, on Ondo State Radio-Vision (OSRV) Programme, 2nd February 1991.

23. Gboyega Ajayi:"The Problems and Challenges of Succession through Elections in Nigeria",in J.O.Arowolo and S.I.Fabarebo (eds): *Nigeria: Contemporary Issues* (Akure:Don Bosco Publishers, 2005) p. 4.

24. Ibid. pp.1-5.

Bibliography

PRIMARY SOURCES

Archival Materials

NAI/SD/M5 – *Muhammed, His Excellency Brigadier M.R.*: Head of the Federal Military Government, Commander-in-Chief of the Armed Forces of the Federal Republic of Nigeria: A Programme for Political Action, 1st October, 1975.

NAI/SD/011 – *Obasanjo, Lt. General Olusegun*; Head of State: Speech at the formal opening of the Command and Staff College, Jaji on Monday 12th September, 1979.

NAI/SD/015 – *Obasanjo, Segun*: Broadcast on the process of military disengagement, 14 July, 1978.

NAI/SD/024 – *Obasanjo, Segun*: Call to Duty – A Collection of Speeches.

NAI/SD/025 – *Obasanjo , Segun*: Towards Civil Rule – Speeches on preparations for changing over to Civilian Government in 1979.

NAI/NC/A7 – Proceeding of the Constituent Assembly, Official report nos. 1-9, 1st November 1977 – 16th December 1978 Vols. I & II.

NAI/NC/A9 – The Constitution of the Federal Republic of Nigeria, 1979.

NAI/NC/A10 – The Presidential System.

NAI/GR/X64 – The Electoral Regulations.

NAI/OX/B48 – Sixteenth IndependenceAniversary Broadcast by His Excellency Lt. General Olusegun Obasanjo, Head of the Federal Military Government, Commander-in-Chief of the Armed Forces – "Transition to Civil Rule" – On Friday October 1st 1976.

NAI/OX/D54 – Indigenisation Degree Explained.

NAI/PX/G7 – 1979 Elections – Fact Sheet on Nigeria.

NAI/PX/G7D – FEDECO Guides.

NAI/PX/G7E – Federal Electoral Commission.

NAI/PX/G7F – The General Elections 1979 – Report by FEDECO.

NAI/A6/A13 – Population Census of Nigeria, 1973 (Lists of Historical Events).

NAI/RG/X58 – 2 Years of President Shagari's Administration – Progress.

NAI/CE/A15B – Adebo, S.O. and 5 others: Second and Final Report of the Wages and Salaries Review together with the White Paper, 1970-71.

NAI/CE/A37A – Government Views on the recommendations of the Technical Committee on Revenue Allocation. (Professor Ojetunji Aboyade) 1978.

NAI/CE/M13A – MARTINS, Col. Msgr. P: Federal Military Government's Views on the Report and Recommendation of the Panel on the Social Implications of the 1975 retirement exercise, by Col. Msgr. p., Martins and Others.

NAI/ CE/XI – Federal Military Government's view on the Report of the Tribunal of Inquiry into the Finances of the 2nd World Black and African Festival of Arts and Culture, 1976.

NAI/MN/X40 – Blueprint for Nigerian Unity.

NAI/SD/A7 – *Adedeji, Dr. Adebayo:* Nigerian's Economic Position Today.

NAI/SN/42 – *Civil War Bulletin:* No Victors, No Vaniquished.

The Nigerian Protectorate Order in Council, 1913

The Nigeria (Legislative Council) Order in Council, 1922

The Nigeria (Legislative Council) Order in Council, 1928

The Nigeria (Legislative Council) (Amendment) Order in Council 1941

Manuscript Collections in Libraries and Research Institutes

a. Africa Leadership Forum (ALF) Abeokuta / Ota
Farm House Dialogue: *Leadership for Development* (Dialogue 1, 13-14 May 1988).

Farm House Dialogue: *Democratic Process in Multi-Nationality* (Dialogue 14, 6-10 February 1991).

Farm House Dialogue: *Economic Democratisation* (Dialogue 16, 14-16 June 1991).

Farm House Dialogue: *Poverty and Democratisation* (Dialogue 18, 20-22 September, 1991).

Farm House Dialogue : *Religious Pluralism and Democracy* (Dialogue 19, 6-8, December 1991).

Farm House Dialogue : *Traditional Institutions and Democracy* (Dialogue 20, 13 January – 2 February, 1992).

Farm House Dialogue: *Democracy and Social Justice* (Dialogue 21, 13-15 March 1992).

Farm House Dialogue: *The Military and Democracy* (Dialogue 22, April/May 1992).

Farm House Dialogue: *Democracy, Institution and Administrative Processes* (Dialogue 23, 19-21 May 1992).

Farm House Dialogue: *Democratic Transition* (Dialogue 24, 3-5 July 1992).

Farm House Dialogue: *Politics and Social Order* (Dialogue 25, 19-21 March 1993).

Farm House Dialogue : *The Military and Society*(Dialogue 27, 23-25 July1993).

b. Friedrich Ebert Foundation (FEF) Lagos

Panel Discussion:" Is there a chance for pluralist democracy in Africa – Is there a chance for Africa without pluralist democracy"? in *International Conference on Democracy in Africa- A New Beginning?* Bonn,1-3 June 1992 (Selected papers and Discussions). Proceedings, One Day Workshop on," Grassroots Political Mobilization in Nigeria" , 15 April, 1992, Better Life Women Center, Ondo.

c. Nigerian Institute of International Affairs (NIIA), Lagos

Ayida, Alison "Before Tomorrow Comes"-Academy Press, Public Lecture.

Ciroma Adamu, "Towards A Stable Third Republic" – National Day Celebration (1989) Public Lecture, in Files on *Nigeria: Politics and Government1966-1993, (NIIA)* Press/Documentation Library.

Momoh, Tony (Prince), 2nd Letter to My Country Man-Corruption in
    High Places.

_____, *4th Letter to My Country Man – Of Poverty and Riches.*
    Proceedings, International Conference on "Nigeria's International
    Economic Relations: Dimensions of Dependence and Change"
    NIIA, Lagos, 9 – 12 December 1986.

Ogunsanwo, Alaba.: " Towards A Stable Third Republic" – National
    Day Celebration (1989) Public Lecture.

*d. Hezekiah Oluwasanmi Library, Obafemi Awolowo University,
Ile – Ife: Manuscripts Collections.*

ECA; African Alternative Framework to Structural Adjustment Pro-
    grammes for Socio-Economic Recovery and Transformation (E/
    ECA/6/Rev.3) (Addis Ababa, 1991).

Federal Government Gazettes, 1966-93

House of Representatives' Debates, 1960-65

Nigeria Year Book, 1966-93.

Senate Parliamentary Debates, 1961.

Private Papers

Annual Reports of the Committee for the Defence of Human Rights
    (CDHR) for the years 1991-1993.

Annual Reports of the Civil Liberties Organisation (CLO) 1987-
    1993.

Freedom Watch - CDHR Monthly Bulletin.

*Victims-*CDHR Newsletter.

Government Publications:

a. *National Electoral Commission (NEC) Abuja*

Federal Republic of Nigeria (FRN): *Report of the Judicial Commis-
    sion of Inquiry into the Affairs of the Federal Electoral Commis-
    sion (FEDECO) 1979-83* (Lagos: Federal Government Printer,
    1991).

NEC: *Report and Recommendations on Party Registration* (Lagos:
    NEC, 1989).

NEC: *Transition to Civil Rule; Laws and Materials on the Electoral
    Process* (Lagos: NEC, 1990).

NEC: *Constitution of the National Republican Convention (NRC),* reproduced for mass circulation by MAMSER, (not dated).

NEC: *The Manifesto of the National Republican Convention (NRC),* Dec. 1989.

NEC: *The Manifesto of the Social Democratic Party (SDP),* Dec. 1989.

NEC: *Proceedings of a Workshop on the Two Party System,* Abuja, 21-24 March 1990.

NEC: *The ABC Of Option A4,* Abuja, 1992.

b. *Mass Mobilization for Social Justice and Economic Recovery (MAMSER) – (Now, National Orientation Agency, NOA), Abuja*

Gana, J.; *Directorate of Social Mobilization: Functions and Programmes of the Directorate* (Lagos: MAMSER, 1987).

FRN:*Report of the Political Bureau* (Lagos: Reproduced by MAMSER, 1987).

_____; *Government's Views and Comments on the Findings and Recommendations of the Political Bureau* (Lagos: MAMSER, 1987).

_____; *Transition to Civil Rule (Political Programme) Decree 19, 1987* (Lagos: MAMSER, 1987).

_____, *Constituent Assembly Decree, 1988* (Lagos: MAMSER, 1988).

FRN; *The Constitution (1989)* reproduced for mass circulation by MAMSER, 1989.

_____; Transition to Civil Rule: Political Programmes (Amendment) Decree 26, 1989 and Political Parties Registration and Activities Decree 27 1989 (Abuja: MAMSER, 1989).

_____; *Report of the Seminar on "Nigeria in Transition"* Kaduna, September 11 – 13, 1989.

_____; *Manifestos of the Social Democratic Party and the National Republican Convention: Some Significant Differences* (Abuja: MAMSER, 1989).

_____; *Political Education Manual: Towards A Free and Democratic Society* (Abuja: MAMSER, 1989).

_____; *How Nigerians Can Save the Naira: A MAMSER Economic Self Reliance Message* (Abuja: MAMSER, 1992).

_____; *Four Years of Social Mobilization: MAMSER in Search of a New Social Order* (Abuja: MAMSER, 1992).

_____; *Towards Excellence in Constitutional Democracy in the Third Republic* (Abuja: MAMSER, 1992).

MAMSER: *Social Transformation for Self Reliance – Proceedings of a National Conference. (Ibadan: Fountain, 1992).*

c. National Population Commission (NPC), Abuja

Address delivered by the Chief of General Staff Vice Admiral Augustus Aikhomu on the occasion of the inauguration of the National Population Commission on 22nd April, 1988.

Welcome Address by Shehu Musa, CFR, Makama Nupe, Chairman, National Population Commission at the Launching of the Public Enlightenment Programme for the 1991 Population Census on 10th May 1990, at the National Assembly Complex, Lagos.

Address delivered by the President, Commander-in-Chief of the Armed Forces, General Ibrahim Badamosi Babangida, CFR, FSS, Mni, at the Launching of the Public Enlightenment programme for the 1991 population census on 10th May 1990, at the National Assembly Complex, Lagos.

SECONDARY SOURCES

Books

Achebe, Chinua; *The Trouble with Nigeria* London: Heinemann, 1984.

Achike, Okay; *Groundwork of Military Law and Military Rule in Nigeria* Enugu: Fourth Dimension Publishers, 1978.

Adamolekun, Ladipo; *The Fall of the Second Republic* Ibadan: Spectrum Books, 1985.

_____; *Politics and Administration in Nigeria* Ibadan:Spectrum Books, 1986.

Adamu, Haroun. and Ogunsanwo, Alaba; *Nigeria; The Making of the Presidential System: 1979 General Elections* Kano: Triumph Publishing Company, 1983.

Adejumobi, Said and Momoh, Abubakar. (eds); *The Political Economy of Nigeria Under Military Rule, 1984 – 1993* Harare: SAPES Books, 1995.

Adekanye, J.Bayo.; *Military Occupation and Social Stratification* Ibadan: Vantage Publishers Ltd., 1993.

Adekanye, J.Bayo, "The Military in the Transition", in Diamond, Larry Kirk-Greene, Anthony and Oyediran, Oyeleye. (eds), *Transition Without End: Nigerian Politics and Civil Society Under Babangida* Ibadan: Vantage Publishers, 1997; pp. 55-80.

_____, "Politics in a Military Context", in Ekeh, P. Peter, Dele-Cole, Patrick. and Olusanya, Gabriel.O. (eds), *Nigeria Since Independence: The First 25 Years Vol. 5 Politics and Constitutions* Ibadan: Heinemann, for Nigeria Since Independence History Project, 1989; pp. 186 – 205.

_____, *The Retired Military as Emergent Power Factor in Nigeria* Ibadan: Heinemann Educational Books (Nigeria) Plc. 1999.

Adekson, J.Bayo; *Nigeria in Search of a Stable Civil-Military System* Aldershot, Boulder: Westview Press, 1981.

Ademoyega, Adewale, *Why We Struck: The Story of the First Nigerian Coup* Ibadan: Evans Brothers, 1981.

Ajayi, 'Gboyega, "The Military-Industrial Complex (MIC) and the Electoral Process in the U.S.: Influence Dynamics in Civil-Military Relationship in an Advanced Democracy", in Ogunba, O. (ed.); *Governance and The Electoral Process: Nigeria and the United States of America* Lagos: Unilag. Press, 1997; pp. 235-249.

Ajayi, 'Gboyega. (ed.); *Critical Perspectives on Nigeria's Socio-Political Development in the 20th Century* (Lagos: Stebak Books, 1999.

Ake, Claude, "The Significance of Military Rule", in *Proceedings of the-National Conference on the Stability of the Third Republic*; Lagos: Concord Group, 1988; pp. 118-130.

Aliyu, A. Yusuf, (ed.); *Return to Civilian Rule* Zaria: ABU, 1982.

Aluko, Olajide, "Politics of Decolonisation in British West Africa, 1945-1960", in Ajayi, J.F.Ade., and Crowder, Micheal. (eds.), *History of West Africa,* Vol. 2, London: Longman, 1974.

Amuwo, Kunle; "The Return of the Military: A Theoretical Construct and Explanation"., in Adejumobi, Said. and Momoh, Abubakar (eds.); *The Political Economy of Nigeria Under Military Rule, 1984-1993* Harare: SAPES Books, 1995; pp. 1-15.

Anifowoshe, R; *Violence and Politics in Nigeria: The Tiv and Yoruba Experience* New York/Enugu: NOK Publication, 1982.

Ayeni, Victor and Soremekun, Kayode (eds.); *Nigeria's Second Republic* Lagos: Daily Times Publications, 1988.

Azikiwe, Nnamdi; *Democracy With Military Vigilance* Nsukka: Africa Book Company, 1974.

Babatope, Ebenezer; *Not His Will: The Awolowo-Obasanjo Wager* Benin City: Jodah Publications, 1990.

Babawale, Tunde; "The Impact of Military Rule on Nigerian Federalism", in Babawale Tunde, Olufemi, Kola and Adewumi, Funmi (eds); *Re-inventing Federalism in Nigeria: Issues and Perspectives* Lagos: Friedrich Ebert Foundation, 1998.; pp. 73-87.

Bechett, P; "Elections and Democracy in Nigeria", in Hayward, F.M. (ed.); *Elections in Independent Africa* Boulder: Westview Press, 1987.

Bienen, Henry; *The Military and Modernisation* Chicago: Aldine 1992.

Biersteker, Thomas.; *Multinationals, the State and Control of the NigerianEconomy* Princeton: Princeton University Press, 1987.

Bretton, H.L.; *Power and Politics in Africa* London: Longman Group, 1973.

Campbell, B.; "Army Reorganization and Military Withdrawal", in Panter-Brick, K. (ed) *Soldiers and Oil.* London: Frank Cass, 1978.

Caron, B., Gboyega, Alex. and Osaghae, E. (eds.); *DemocraticTransition in Africa* Ibadan: CREDU, 1992.

Carr, E.H., *What is History?* (Middlesex: Penguin Books, 1964).

Cohen, Robin; *Labour and Politics in Nigeria* London: Heinemann, 1974.

Coleman, James S., *Background to Nigerian Nationalism* Berkely: University of California Press, 1958.

Crowder, Michael; *The Story of Nigeria* London: Faber & Faber, 1966.

Dare, L.O., *The Praetorian Trap: The Problems and Prospects of Military Disengagement* – Inaugural Lecture, O.A.U., Ile-Ife 1989.

Davidson, Basil.; *The Blackman's Burden* Ibadan: Spectrum Books, 1992.

Decalo, Samuel; *Coups and Army Rule in Africa: Studies in Military Style* New Haven: Yale University Press, 1968.

Deutsch, Karl, *Politics and Government, 2nd ed.* Boston: Houghton Mifflin Company, 1974.

Diamond, Larry; *Class, Ethnicity and Democracy in Nigeria: The Failure of the First Republic* Londres: Macmillan, 1988.

_____; "Nigeria: Pluralism, Statism and theStruggle for Democracy", in Diamond, L; Linz, J.L. and Lipset, S.M. (eds);*Democracy in Developing Countries* Boulder: Lynne Rienner, 1988.

Dudley, Billy. J.; *Instability and Political Order: Politics and Crises in Nigeria* Ibadan: Ibadan University Press, 1973.

_____; *An Introduction to Nigerian Government and Politics* London: Macmillan Publishers Ltd., 1982.

_____; *Parties and Politics in Northern Nigeria* London: Frank Cass & Co. Ltd., 1968.

_____; "The Military and Politics in Nigeria", in Doorn, V. (ed.), *Military Profession and Military Regimes* The Hague: Mouton & Co. Pub., 1969.

Ekeh, Peter, Dele-Cole, Patrick, Olusanya, Gabriel O. (eds.); *Nigeria Since Independence: The First 25 Years, Politics and Constitutions, Vol. V.* Ibadan: Heinemann Nig., 1989.

Ekekwe, Eme; *Class and State in Nigeria* Lagos: Longman Nig. Ltd., 1986.

Elaigwu, John. I.; *Gowon* Ibadan: Westbooks, 1985.

Ezera, Kalu, *Constitutional Developments in Nigeria* London: Ind. Ed., 1964.

Fadahunsi, Akin and Babawale, Tunde (eds) *Nigeria: Beyond Structural Adjustment* Lagos: Friedrich Ebert Foundation, 1996.

Falola, Toyin, Ajayi, A. Alao, A. and Babawale, B. *The Military Factor in Nigeria, 1966-1985* New York: The Edwin Mellen Press, 1994.

Falola, Toyin and Ihonvbere, Julius; *The Rise and Fall of Nigeria's Second Republic, 1979-1984* London: Zed Books, 1984.

Fawehinmi, Gani; *June 12 Crisis: The Illegality of Shonekan's Government* Lagos: Nigerian Law Publications, 1993.

Feld, M.D., *The Structure of Violence: Armed Forces and Social Systems* Beverly Hills: Sage Publications, 1997.

Finer, Samuel E., *The Man on Horseback: The Role of The Military in Politics, 2nd ed.* London: Peregrine Books, 1976.

First, Ruth; *The Barrel of a Gun: Political Power in Africa* London: Allen Lane, 1970.

Gutteridge, William.F.; *Military Regimes in Africa* (Londres: Methuen Press, 1975).

Harbeson, John. (ed.); *The Military in African Politics* New York: Praeger, 1987.

Huntington, Samuel P. *Political Order in Changing Societies* New Haven, Connecticut: Yale University Press, 1968.

Hutchful, Eboe, "Military Issues in the Transition to Democracy", in Hutchful, Eboe. and Bathily, A, (eds.), *The Military and Militarism in Africa* Dakar: COESRIA, 1998.

Ikoku, Sam. G. *Nigeria's Fourth Coup D'Etat* Enugu: Fourth Dimension Publishers, 1985.

Jakande, Lateef.Kayode., *The Trial of Obafemi Awolowo* London: Secker and Warbury, 1966.

Janowitz, Morris, *The Military in the Political Development of New Nations: An Essay in Comparative Analysis* Chicago: Phoenix Books, 1964.

Jemibewon, David. M.; *A Combatant in Government* Ibadan: Heinemann, 1978.

Johnson, John J., *The Role of the Military in Underdeveloped Countries* Princeton, N. J.: Princeton University Press, 1962.

Joseph, Richard A.; *Democracy and Prebendal Politics In Nigeria: The Rise and Fall of the Second Republic* Ibadan: Spectrum Books Ltd., 1991.

Kirk-Greene, Anthony. and Rimmer, Douglas; *Nigeria Since 1970: A Political And Economic Outline* London: Hodder and Stoughton, 1981.

Kurfi, Ahmadu; *The Nigerian General Elections, 1959 and 1979, and the Aftermath* Lagos: Macmillan Nigerian Publishers, 1983.

Luckman, Robin; *The Nigerian Military: A Sociological Analysis of Authority and Revolt, 1960- 67* Cambridge: Cambridge University Press, 1971.

Madunagu, Edwin; *Nigeria: The Economy and the People – The Political Economy of State Robbery and Its Popular Democratic Negation* London: New Beacon Books, 1984.

Marx, Karl; *Capital*, Vol. 1, Moscow: Progress Publishers, 1974.

Miles, W.; *Election in Nigeria: A Grassroots Perspective* Boulder:Lynne Reinner, 1988.

Mimiko, Nazeem.O. (ed.); *Crisis and Contradictions in Nigeria's Democratisation Programme, 1986 – 1993* Akure: Stebak Ventures, 1995.

Mohammed, A.S. and Edoh, T. (eds.); *Nigeria: A Republic In Ruins* Zaria: Department of Political Science, ABU, 1986.

Miners, N.J., *The Nigerian Army, 1956 – 1966* London:Methuen, 1971.

Nnoli, Okwudiba; *Ethnic Politics in Nigeria* Enugu: Fourth Dimension Publishers, 1978.

Nwabueze, Benjamin O.; *A Constitutional History of Nigeria* Londres: C. Hurst, 1982.

_____;*The Presidential Constitution of Nigeria* Londres: C. Hurst, 1982.

_____; Nigeria's *Presidential Constitution, 1979-83: The Second Experiment in Constitutional Democracy* London: Longman, 1985.

Nwankwo, Arthur; *The Military Option to Democracy* Enugu: Fourth Dimension Publishers, 1987.

_____; *Civilianised Soldiers: Army-Civilian Government for Nigeria* Enugu: Fourth Dimension Publishing Company Ltd.; 1984.

Nzeribe, Francis A.; *Nigeria: Another Hope Betrayed: The Second Coming of the Nigerian Military* London: Kilimajaro, 1985.

Obasanjo, Olusegun; *My Command* Lagos: Heinemann Educational Books, 1980.

_____; *Not My Will* Ibadan: University Press Ltd., 1990.

_____; and Shyllon, F.; *The Demise of the Rule of Law in Nigeria Under the Military: Two Points of View* Ibadan: Institute of African Studies, 1980.

Odetola, Olatunde; *Military Politics in Nigeria: Economic Development And Political Stability* New Brumswick, N.J.: Transaction Books, 1978.

_____; *Military Regimes and Development: A Comparative Analysis in African Societies* London: George Allen and Unwin, 1982.

Ojiako, James O; *13 Years of Military Rule* Lagos: Daily Times Publications, 1979.

_____; *Nigeria: Yesterday, Today and ...?* Onitsha: Africa Educational Publishers, 1981.

Ojo, Afolabi; *Constitutional Law and Military Rule in Nigeria* Ibadan: Evans Brothers Nigeria Ltd., 1987.

Okoye, Mokugwo, *A Letter to Dr. Nnamdi Azikiwe* Enugu: Fourth Dimension Publishers, 1979.

Olagunju, Olatunji. and Oyovbaire, Samuel E.; *Portrait of a New Nigeria: Selected Speeches of IBB Vol. 1* Lagos: Precision Press, n.d..

_____; *For Their Tomorrow We Gave Our Today: Selected Speeches of IBB Vol. II* Ibadan: Safari Books Export Ltd.,1993.

Olorode, Omotoye, Raji, W. Ogunye, J. and Jegede, S. (eds.); *Non-Governmental Organisations (NGOS) and Democracy* Lagos: CHDR, 1997.

Olugbemi, Stephen O. (ed); *Alternative Political Future for Nigeria* Lagos: NPSA, 1985.

Oluleye, James J.; *Military Leadership in Nigeria, 1966-1979* Ibadan: University Press Ltd.; 1985.

Olusanya, Gabriel O., "The Nationalist Movement in Nigeria", in Ikime, Obaro (ed.), *Groundwork of Nigerian History* London: Heinemann, 1980.

Oyediran, Oyeleye; *Survey of Nigerian Affairs* Lagos: NIIA, 1978.

Oyeweso, Siyan (ed.); *Perspectives on the Nigerian Civil war* Lagos: Campus Press, 1992.

Oyovbaire, Sam. and Olagunju, Tunji. (eds.); *Foundations of a New Nigeria: The IBB Era* Lagos: Precision Press, n.d..

Panter-Brick,Keith. (ed.); *Nigerian Politics and Military Rule: Prelude To Civil War* Londres: Althone Press, 1970.

_____; (ed.); *Soldiers and Oil: The Political Transformation of Nigeria* London: Frank Cass, 1978.

Peil, Margaret, *Nigerian Politics: The Peoples' View* London: Cassell and Company Ltd., 1976.

Rappopport, David C., "A Comparative Theory of Military and Political Types" in Huntington, S.P. (ed.) *Changing Patterns of Military Politics* New York: Free Press, 1962; pp.71– 101.

Sabine, George and Thorson, Thomas, *A History of Political Theory, 4th ed.* Illinois: Dryden Press, 1973.

Sandbrook, Richard, *The Politics of African Economic Stagnation* Cambridge: Cambridge University Press, 1983.

Schwarz, F.A.O.., *Nigeria: The Tribes, the Nation or the Race* Cambridge: Massachusetts Institute of Technology Press, 1965.

Shills, Edward A.; *Political Development in the New States* The Hague: Monton & Co., 1962.

Sklar, R.; *Nigerian Political Parties: Power In an Emergent African Nation* Princeton, N.J.: Princeton University Press, 1963.

Sunmonu, Hassan A., *Trade Unionism in Nigeria: Challenges for the 21ˢᵗ Century* Lagos: Friedrich Ebert Foundation, 1996.

Tamuno, T.N., *The Evolution of the Nigerian State: The Southern Phase, 1898 – 1914* Ibadan: Longman, 1978.

Tyoden, S.G. (ed.); *Transition to Civil Rule: The Journey So Far* Lagos: NPSA, 1992.

Usman, Yusuf. Bala; *For the Liberation of Nigeria: Essays and Lectures, 1969 – 1978* London: New Beacon Books, 1979.

_____; *Political Repression in Nigeria* Zaria: Gaskiya Corporation, 1982.

_____; *The Manipulation of Religion in Nigeria, 1977-1987* Kaduna: Vanguard Publishers, 1987.

Welch, Claude (ed.); *The Soldier and State in Africa: A Comparative Analysis of Military Intervention and Political Change* Evanston: North Western University Press, 1970.

Williams, Gavin; *State and Society in Nigeria* Idanre: Afrografika Publishers, 1980.

World Bank; *The Nigerian Structural Adjustment Programme: Policies, Impact and Prospects* Washington, D.C.,1988.

Zik: *Selected Speeches of Dr. Nnamdi Azikiwe* Oxford: Oxford University Press, 1961.

Articles in Journals and Other Periodicals

Adekanye , J. Bayo; "Nigerian Armed Forces and the Conduct of Elections",*Quarterly Journal of Administration,* XXIII (1 & 2) October 1988 – January 1989; pp. 27-38.

_____; "Elections in Nigeria: Problems, Strategies and Options", *Nigerian Journal of Electoral and Political Behaviour*, 1(i), 1990,; pp. 1-4.

_____, "The Military as a Problem in Comparative Political Analysis", *Nigerian Journal of International Affairs,* XVIII (i) 1992,; pp. 1-28.

_____; "Military Organisation and Federal Society", in *Quarterly Journal of Administration* XVI (1 & 2), 1981/82; pp. 3-23.

_____, "Machiavelli and the Military: The Prince and the Psychology of Empty Power", in *Strategic Studies* (Islamabad) III(2), 1985.; pp. 9-36.

_____, "Towards Explaining Civil-Military Instability in Contemporary Africa: A Comparative Political Mode", in *Current Research on Peace and Violence*, 8(3x4) 1978.; pp. 191-206.

_____, "Pay, Promotion and Other Self-Regarding Interests of Military Intervention in Politics ", in *Military Affairs*, 45(1) 1981.; pp. 18-22.

Adetoro, John B.; "The Indigenisation of Foreign Enterprises", in *Nigerian Journal of International Affairs*, 1(i), July 1975,; pp. 32-38.

Ajayi, 'Gboyega.; "Government and Religious Patronage in Contemporary Nigeria, 1980-1989: Implications for the stability of the Nation", *Zeitchrift fur Afrikastuden (ZAST)* 7 / 8, 1990,; pp. 56-65.

_____; "The Military as a Corrective Agency: How Realistic?" *Glamour*, II (i) October 1995,; pp. 16-17.

Ake, Claude; "Rethinking African Democracy", *Journal of Democracy* Winter 1991,; pp. 32-44.

Alao, Akin; "The Civil Society in Nigeria" *Glamour*, II (i), October, 1995,; pp. 18.

Amuwo, Kunle; "The Nigerian Military as a New Class", in *Proceedings of the 16th Annual Conference of the Nigerian Political Science Association, 1989, Section 7*,; pp. 2-10.

Babawale, Tunde; "Nigeria's Search for Alternatives: Notes on the Limited Possibilities of Democracy in the Third Republic", *ZAST*, (5), 1989,; pp. 49-57.

_____; "The Military State, Intra-Elite Conflicts and Industrial Democracy in Nigeria", *Journal of Arts and Social Sciences*, 1(i), January 1996,; pp. 48-59.

Dare, L.O., "Military Withdrawal from Politics in Nigeria", in *International Political Science Review*, 3, 1981.; pp. 51-62.

Diamond, Larry; "Nigeria's Search for a New Political Order" in *Journal of Democracy*, Spring 1991,; pp. 54-59.

Flynn, Peter, "Class, Clientelism and Coercion: Some Mechanisms of Internal Dependency and Control", in *Journal of Commonwealth and Comparative Studies* 22(I), 1980.

Grundy, Kenneth: "Negative Image of African Military", in *Review of Politics* XXX (October 1968); pp. 429-439.

Ihonvbere, Julius O.; "Structural Adjustment and Nigeria's Democratic Transition", in *Trans-Africa Forum* VIII (3) Fall 1999,pp. 61-83.

_____; "Nigeria as Africa's Great Power: Constraints and Prospects for the 1990s", *International Journal*, XLVI, Summer 1991,; pp. 510-535.

Sandbrook, Richard, "Patrons, Clients and Factions: New Dimensions of Conflict Analysis in Africa", in *Canadian Journal of Political Science*, 5(1), 1972.

Scott, James C., "Patron-Client Politics and Political Change in South East Asia", in *American Political Science Review*, 61 (1), 1972.

Taiwo, Olufemi., "Political Obligation and Military Rule", in *The Philosophical Forum* XXVIII (2), Winter 1996.; pp. 161-193.

Nwokeji, G. Ugochukwu, "Ojukwu's Leadership and the Nigerian Civil War, 1967-70: An Analysis of the Role of the Individual in History", *Ife Journal of History*, II (i) 1995,; pp. 71-89.

Oyediran, Oyeleye; "The Gospel of the Second Chance: A Comparison of Obasanjo and Babangida Military Disengagement in Nigeria", *Quarterly Journal of Administration* XXIII (1&2) October 1988-January 1989.

Perlmutter, Amos; "The Praetorian State and the Praetorian Army: Toward a Taxonomy of Civil Military Relations in Developing Countries", *Comparative Politics*, I (3), April 1969,; pp. 382-405.

Signed Articles in Newspapers

Dada, P.A. and Alao, A.; "The ABN's Pandora Box", in *Sunday Tribune*, 25 July 1993,; pp. 8 and 9.

Ibrahim, F. O.; "IBB's Year of Destiny", in *Daily Times*, 1ˢᵗ January 1993,; pp. 11.

Idaye, Braimah; "The Abiola Issue", in *Sunday Concord*, 24 March, 1996,; pp. 9.

Signed Article in an Encyclopedia

Dahl, Robert A.; "Power", in *International Encyclopedia of the Social Sciences*, 1968 ed. S.V.

Unsigned Article in an Encyclopedia

"Militarism ", in *International Encyclopedia of the Social Sciences*, 1968 ed. S.V.

UNPUBLISHED SOURCES

Unpublished Thesis/Dissertation

Adejumobi, Said, "The Military as Economic Manager: The Babangida Regime and the Structural Adjustment Programme". Unpublished Ph.D Thesis, University of Ibadan, Ibadan, 1999.

Akande, Adeolu O., "Machiavellian Statecraft, Corporatism and Neo-Patrimonial Rule: Nigeria Under General Ibrahim Babangida". Unpublished Ph.D Thesis, University of Ibadan, Ibadan, 1997.

Johnson, Eno, "A Comparative Study of Selected Broadcast Speeches of Civilian and Military Heads of Government In Nigeria". Unpublished Ph.D Thesis, University of Ibadan, Ibadan, 1988.

Osoba, Samuel Olusegun, "The Colonial Antecedents and Contemporary Development of Nigeria's Foreign Policy: A Study in the History of Social, Economic and Political Conflict". Unpublished Ph.D Thesis, Moscow State University, Moscow, 1967.

Unpublished Conference Papers

Ciroma, M.A.; "Military Intervention in National Politics (II)", *Aborted National Conference on the Alternative to SAP* Organized by the National Consultative Forum (NCF), Lagos, September 1990.

CHDR; "The National Agenda on Democracy" *Ibid.*

Jemibewon, D.M.; "Military Intervention in National Politics (1)", *Ibid.*

Mustapha, A. R.; "Parties, the Transitional Programme and Democracy in Nigeria", *Ibid.*

NANS; "Pre-conditions for Stable Democratic Culture", *Ibid.*

Draft Manuscripts

Ajayi, G.; "The Military Factor in Nigeria's Power Politics".

_____ ; "The 'Mad Dog' Syndrome and the Caging of the Civil Society in Nigeria".

Akorede, V.E.A.; "Military Regimes and the Politics of Revenue Allocation in Nigeria".

NEWSPAPERS AND MAGAZINES

African Concord (Lagos) 1987-1996.

African Guardian (Lagos) 1986-1993.

African Report (London) 1965.

African Today (London) 1998.

Daily Sketch (Ibadan) 1985-1993.

Daily Times (Lagos) 1966-1993.

Hotline (Kaduna) 1993.

National Concord (Lagos) 1986-1993.

Newswatch (Lagos) 1985-1997.

Nigerian Tribune (Ibadan) 1975-1993.

Punch (Lagos) 1985-1997.

Sunday Tribune (Ibadan) 1978-1998.

Tell (Lagos) 1992-1998.

Tempo (Lagos) 1992-1997.

The Guardian (Lagos) 1985-1993.

The News (Lagos) 1993-1997.

Vanguard (Lagos) 1985-1997.

West Africa (London) 1966 - 1993.

Index